Weird, Wacky and Wild
TENNESSEE TRIVIA

J. Ernest Nolan & Lisa Wojna

BLUE BIKE BOOKS

© 2010 by Blue Bike Books

All rights reserved. No part of this work covered by the copyrights hereon may be reproduced or used in any form or by any means—graphic, electronic or mechanical—without the prior written permission of the publisher, except for reviewers, who may quote brief passages. Any request for photocopying, recording, taping or storage on information retrieval systems of any part of this work shall be directed in writing to the publisher.

The Publisher: Blue Bike Books Ltd.
Website: www.bluebikebooks.com

Library and Archives Canada Cataloguing in Publication

Nolan, J. Ernest, 1970–
Tennessee trivia / J. Ernest Nolan and Lisa Wojna.

ISBN 978-1-926700-26-7

1. Tennessee—Miscellanea. I. Wojna, Lisa, 1962– II. Title.

F436.6.N65 2010   976.8   C2010-900576-7

Project Director: Nicholle Carrière
Project Editor: Jordan Allan
Cover Image: © Geir-Olav Lyngfell | iStockPhoto.com and Photos.com
Illustrations: Craig Howrie, Roger Garcia, Peter Tyler, Roly Wood

We acknowledge the support of the Alberta Foundation for the Arts for our publishing program.

We acknowledge the financial support of the Government of Canada.
Nous reconnaissons l'appui financier du gouvernement du Canada.

PC: 40

DEDICATION

To Davy Crockett, the King of the Wild Frontier and hero of the Battle of the Alamo.

CONTENTS

INTRODUCTION 7
WELCOME TO TENNESSEE
   Symbols of the State 8
   Inanimate State Symbols 12
   Living (or Previously Living) State Symbols 20
   Tennessee at a Glance 26

ENVIRONMENTALLY SPEAKING
   Geography 37
   Weather and Climate 42
   Amazing Animals 44
   Amphibian Mania 48
   Wooden Wonders 54
   Mountain Bogs 57

STATE FOUNDATIONS
   The Founding of Tennessee 59
   Founding Fathers and Historic Heroes 63
   Tennessee and the Civil War 72

HISTORY AND CULTURE
   Spiritual State: Religion in Tennessee 76
   Timeline of Tennessee's Civil Rights History 82
   History on the Map 86
   The Tennessee Valley Authority 92
   Oak Ridge and the Birth of the Bomb 93

THE ARTS IN TENNESSEE
   Tennessee Art Museums 97
   A State of Letters 101

COUNTRY, BLUES, SOUL AND ROCK 'N' ROLL
   A Brief History of Country Music 105
   Six Legends of Country Music 108
   Men and Women of the Memphis Blues 114
   Memphis: City of Soul 121
   Sun Records: The Cradle of Rock 'n' Roll 127

FROM SCREEN TO CANVAS
Tennessee's Top Television and Screen Stars 132
Tennessee and the Visual Arts 137
Tennessee's Legendary Ladies 143

TOP SIGHTS AND SITES
Tennessee's Architectural Icons 148
Famous Tennessee Landmarks 154
Roadside Attractions 158

SPORTS
Tennessee's Top Teams 161

STATE OF THE CLASSROOM
Tennessee Schools' Report Card 168
Tennessee Colleges and Universities 170

TENNESSEE COMMUNITIES
What's in a Name? 178
Origins of Tennessee Counties 182
County Curiosities 192

EAT, DRINK AND BE MERRY
Numbing Numbers and Nuggets 205
Sex and the Law 208
Gay Couples by the Numbers 210
Tennessee on Tap 211
Tennessee Eats 215
Tennessee Whiskey 217

LAST BUT NOT LEAST 221
TEN REASONS TO MOVE TO TENNESSEE 221

ACKNOWLEDGEMENTS

I'd like to thank Jordan Allan for his clear-headed suggestions. I'd also like to thank Taryn Simpson and Yvonne Perry for their advice, and Liz Coleman at the Nashville Public Library for her assistance on this deep, lengthy and rigorous gathering of all things trivial in the Volunteer State.

–J. Ernest

Many thanks to our clever editor, who pieced together the work of two authors and did so seamlessly; to my co-author, Joe; and to my family—my husband Garry, sons Peter, Matthew and Nathan, daughters Melissa and Jada, and grandson Seth. Without you, all this and anything else I do in my life would be meaningless.

–Lisa

INTRODUCTION

The state of Tennessee is many things to many people. For some, Tennessee is the state they associate with country music and Southern living. For others, Tennessee was a border state of the Confederacy and one of the bloodiest of the Civil War. Tennessee was the site of the some of the most progressive struggles during the Civil Rights Movement of the '60s. Tennessee is also the state where Dr. Martin Luther King Jr. was assassinated. Tennessee has become known as a "red" state in recent national elections, but Al Gore—a hero to the Democratic Party and to true blue liberal voters in America—hails from the state of Tennessee. Tennesseans like Davy Crockett lived bold lives full of adventure and discovery as early settlers to the area. However, many of the Native Americans who originally called Tennessee home later found themselves expelled from its beautiful surroundings, walking a path that is now known as the Trail of Tears.

Tennessee is a state that boasts mountains to the east, a basin in the center and the Mississippi River to the west, and just as the landscape of the state refuses to conform to one type of terrain, the history of the place and the character of its people also refuse easy definitions and convenient labels. Tennessee has been my adopted home for nearly 18 years, and it's my hope that this fun, informative volume will treat this place as well as it has treated me.

SYMBOLS OF THE STATE

What's in a Name?

It's fitting that the word "Tennessee" is of Native American origin, as it was the American Indians who were the first to open up the land to the west of the Carolinas. European settlers followed close behind, and in the summer of 1567, Spanish explorer Captain Juan Pardo led an expedition through the region. Captain Pardo is believed to be the first person to have recorded the name "Tennessee," referring to the land he was traveling through. It is thought that the name was borrowed from a Cherokee village called Tanasqui-Tennessee.

As prescient as Captain Pardo was in choosing the name Tennessee, it wasn't until Andrew Jackson came along in the 1750s and the state joined the Union in 1796 that Tennessee was entered as the official state name. The current spelling has evolved, and over its history, there have been numerous renditions of the name in public documents, including Tanase, Tunesee, Tonice, Tenasi, Tennesy and Tennassee.

Meaning, Anyone?

Most sources agree on one thing—the actual meaning of the word "Tennessee" has been lost to history. However, there are still many theories. One source suggests that the name originated in the Creek language, then was modified by the Cherokee and used in the naming of their village, Tanasqui-Tennessee. Another source suggests that the word "Tennessee" comes from the Yuchi language and means "meeting place." And Tennessee historian Samuel Cole Williams makes yet another proposal, saying that the name may have referred to "the bends" of a river, though other historians have since disputed this idea.

Also Known As...

Every state has a nickname or two, but Tennessee has quite the collection to brag about. Probably the most popular of them is the moniker the "Volunteer State." While there's probably no end of volunteers living in Tennessee today, the name actually refers to the abundance of volunteer soldiers that joined Andrew Jackson's army during the War of 1812.

Tennessee was also home to three presidents in a very short span of time. Andrew Jackson served from 1829 to 1837, James Knox Polk reigned in the big chair from 1845 to 1849 and Vice President Andrew Johnson took over the presidency after the assassination of Abraham Lincoln in 1865 and served until 1869. With that kind of track record, it's no wonder the state was bestowed the nickname the "Mother of Southwestern Statesmen."

From 1830 to 1840, Tennessee was well known for its production of pork and corn products, hence the "Hog and Hominy State" nickname. Another popular nickname is the "Big Bend State," referring to the Samuel Cole Williams' suggestion that the name Tennessee refers to the "big bend" of the Tennessee River.

DID YOU  KNOW?

Andrew Jackson was hailed a hero of the War of 1812. He was the seventh president of the United States and the first president to come from Tennessee. He was a tad on the tough side, though, hence his nickname, "Old Hickory." He was also the first president to face an assassination attempt—two assassins, at different times, pulled pistols on Jackson, but both misfired.

Making It Official
Tennessee was the 16th state to be admitted to the Union. It was officially declared a state in 1796.

The Simple Truth

"Tennessee—America at Its Best." Those few words say it all when it comes to how Tennesseans feel about their home. The Tennessee General Assembly chose those words as the state's official slogan in 1965.

Guiding Principles

In 1987, the state of Tennessee adopted its state motto, "Agriculture and Commerce." The words were taken from Tennessee's state seal.

If You're From Here

Those of us lucky enough to hail from Tennessee are often called "Tennesseans." We're also called "Big Benders," after the popular theory that "Tennessee" means "big bend." The moniker "Butternuts" might need a little more explanation, but when it was originally bestowed on folks from the Volunteer State, it made a lot more sense. The nickname was first used during the American Civil War and referred to the tan-colored uniforms worn by Tennessee soldiers. The term Butternuts, therefore, first referred only to the soldiers, but was gradually applied to everyone else who lived in Tennessee.

DID YOU KNOW?

Zachary Taylor is a popular name when it comes to U.S. political figures. Not only was it the name of the country's 12th president, it was also the name of a U.S. Republican representative voted into the 49th Congress and who served from March 4, 1885, to March 3, 1887—*that* Zachary Taylor was born in Tennessee on May 9, 1849.

Seal of Approval

The Constitution of the State of Tennessee acknowledged the first rendition of the state seal in 1796. Along with the words "The Great Seal of the State of Tennessee"—which surround the seal's outer edge—there is a plow, a sheaf of wheat and a cotton plant in the center of the upper portion. A boat, which once also held a boatman, is found on the bottom half of the seal—the later versions of the seal removed the boatman. The words "agriculture" and "commerce," along with the date the seal was adopted, February 6, 1796, and Roman numerals XVI, were also on the original seal, though the current version only sports the year of its adoption and not the complete date. It wasn't until 1987 that the Tennessee General Assembly officially adopted a standardized state seal.

WELCOME TO TENNESSEE

INANIMATE STATE SYMBOLS

Flying High

Tennessee's state flag is simple in its design, but rich with meaning. The majority of the main body of the flag is a solid red. This, according to LeRoy Reeves, the flag's designer, was meant to signify the fact that "Tennesseans are true-blooded Americans." The center of the flag has a blue circle bordered in white, with three white stars in its middle. The color white is meant to symbolize purity, and the color blue represents "the love that Tennesseans feel for their state." The far right border of the flag is edged with a wide ribbon of blue and a narrow ribbon of white. This appears to be the only design element chosen solely for its aesthetic purposes.

The number three is also significant in the design: the flag has three stars, three colors and three sections. Reeves, a member of the Third Regiment of the Tennessee Infantry, told the Tennessee state legislature that the three stars represented "the three grand divisions of the state," referring to the Great Smoky Mountains and hills of East Tennessee, the Cumberland Plateau in the center of the state and the cotton-growing fields of the western portion. He went on to explain that the stars are "bound together by the endless circle of the blue field, the symbol being three bound together in one—an indissoluble trinity." The Tennessee state legislature officially adopted Reeves' design as the new state flag on April 17, 1905.

 It's not official as far as the state legislature goes, but in 1939, the Tennessee General Assembly did ask the U.S. War Department to design a Flag of the Governor. They ended up with a hickory tree with three white stars—which is, in effect, the crest of the Tennessee National Guard—centered

on a solid red background, a single white star beaming in from each corner.

Sing Loud, Sing Proud

Tennessee is serenaded "From the Smokie Mountain mornings to the Mississippi shores" in "The Pride of Tennessee." The 99th General Assembly adopted the song—written by Fred Congdon, Thomas Vaughn and Carol Elliot—as the state's official song in 1996. Aside from hailing the beauty of the state, the song also draws attention to what's most important to Tennesseans: "Yes courage, faith and vision are the pride of Tennessee."

But Tennesseans are apparently a musical bunch as this song is far from the first one they've embraced as their state song. In 1925, the 64th General Assembly adopted "My Homeland, Tennessee" as their official song. Nell Grayson Taylor wrote the words, saluting their "Dear homeland, Tennessee," and Roy Lamont Smith composed the music.

Ten years later, the 69th General Assembly adopted "When it's Iris Time in Tennessee" as the state's official song, written and composed by Willa Waid Newman. As with every state song, Tennessee's beauty was extolled as being beyond that of any other state, a land where "the mockingbird sings at the break of day," bringing with it memories of "when it's iris time in Tennessee."

By 1965, the 84th General Assembly decided that a change was again in order, and they adopted yet another new song, the "Tennessee Waltz," composed by Redd Stewart and Pee Wee King. The song's two verses tell a rather sad tale of how a beau and his girl were dancing to the Tennessee Waltz. After introducing his darling to an old pal, the gent singing the song finds himself alone as his girl leaves with his friend.

The "Tennessee Waltz" hung in there as the official song until husband-and-wife team Boudleaux and Felice Bryant wrote the country-bluegrass song "Rocky Top." The song, which salutes a unique way of life with "no telephone bills" but where you can find a "moonshine still" and "corn from a jar," was adopted in 1982.

In 1992, the great state of Tennessee was being serenaded in the song "Tennessee," whose words and music were written by Vivian Rorie. This musical salute to the state was adopted as the state song of the 97th General Assembly in that year, and although it's not technically a "state song," Tennesseans certainly regarded it as such.

As a way to capture the imagination of a younger generation, teach a little history and have a little fun with the entire enterprise, an official bicentennial rap was adopted in 1996. Joan Hill Hanks of Signal Mountain composed the rap "TENNE-, TENNE-, TENNES-SEE!" The rap highlights Tennessee's geography, its people, the success stories and its cultural diversity, and at the end of it all, it shouts, "Birthday wishes on 200 years—Give Tennessee a big, big, cheer!"

Now that's the way to host a party!

Nothing Prettier than a Poem

If you're a little too shy to try to belt out your love for your state in song, how about reciting a sweet salute? In 1973, the 88th General Assembly adopted the poem "Oh Tennessee, My Tennessee" as the state's official poem. Written by Vice Admiral William Lawrence, the poem describes the natural beauty of the state and the love he felt for his homeland. It's perhaps one of the most poignant salutes to Tennessee ever penned, written over a 60-day period in which then-Commander Lawrence was locked away in solitary confinement—those 60 days represented just a small portion of the officer's six years as a prisoner of war in North Vietnam, from 1967 to 1973. The love he felt for his homeland, spelled out in the words of his poem, must have become like a mantra for him. Knowing his story, one can imagine the longing he was feeling for the home he so vividly described in the last four lines:

> *And O'er the World as I May Roam,*
> *No Place Exceeds my Boyhood Home.*
> *And Oh How Much I Long to See*
> *My Native Land, My Tennessee.*

I Am Tennessee

In 1987, the 95th General Assembly made a special commendation to Major Hooper Penuel for writing a declamation in honor of Governor Ned R. McWherter's inauguration. The Tennessee General Assembly further recognized Penuel's efforts by making his words the official state declamation.

Flying High

The Tennessee Museum of Aviation, which also includes the Tennessee Aviation Hall of Fame, is the state's official salute to aeronautics. The museum was given statewide recognition when it first opened on December 15, 2001. It has a 35,000-square-foot aircraft hangar, a gallery, a gift shop, offices and a ton of storage space. Another 45,000-square-foot area, adjacent to the Gatlinburg-Pigeon Forge Airport, contains an aircraft ramp area.

DID YOU KNOW?

Not only does the average Tennessean have an appreciation for the arts, but the state has even named an official fine art. In 1981, porcelain painting was given that honor.

Swing Your Partner...

In 1980, the square dance was named Tennessee's official state dance. According to the *Tennessee Blue Book*, the dance was chosen because of its resilience: "Among the traditions (of our ancestors) that have survived intact is the Square Dance, a uniquely attractive art form that remains a vibrant and entertaining part of Tennessee folklore." So, the next time you're looking for a night out on the town, why not try a heel and toe and a do-si-do.

Party Time!

Smithville, Tennessee, is home to only about 4000 residents, but man, do they know how to throw a party! On the first weekend of every July, the town hosts the Fiddlers' Jamboree and Craft Festival. About 80,000 people attend the two-day event, which was first held in 1972. Initially, townsfolk thought the jamboree would be a perfect way to celebrate the Independence Day holiday, but it's grown to such an extent that, in 1997, it was recognized as the state's official jamboree and crafts festival.

Tennessee Tartan

The Scottish influence on Tennesseans was recognized in 1999 when the state adopted the tartan worn by the Heart of Tennessee Scottish Celebration and other Scottish societies as their official tartan. Dark greens, purples and blues interspersed with lines of red and white make this tartan really pop.

Quick now, I bet you can answer this question: name two heroes of the Texas Revolution with connections to Tennessee? If you answered Davy Crockett and Sam Houston, then you're right! Both heroes have been touted for generations as examples of the courageous Tennessee spirit.

Beauty and Age

The oldest gem known to man has a special place of honor for Tennesseans. In 1979, the pearl was named Tennessee's official gemstone. What folklorists have called "teardrops of the moon" apparently fell throughout the Volunteer State, scattering themselves in streams "from the Pigeon and Holston in the east to the Forked Deer and Obion in the west," as the *Tennessee Blue Book* explains it. After church on lazy Sunday afternoons, youngsters used to pick mussels from these many streams and pluck pearls of all colors and shapes from their clamped shells. This was especially popular between 1882 and 1914, when the waters of the Caney Fork in Middle Tennessee were particularly rich with these pearl-bearing mussels.

Sadly, after World War I, dams were constructed on several of these rivers, changing the depth and flow of the waters and affecting the overall water quality. The mussels suffered, and although you can still find pearl-bearing mussels in Tennessee, harvesting them is more of a hobby than a profitable business venture. Still, the pearl made a big impression on Tennessee's history and has rightfully earned a place as one of the state's symbols.

No Argument Here

Just in case there was any doubt, English is the official language of Tennessee. It received this status in 1984.

Chug-a-chug

Move aside, Thomas the Tank Engine—this cartoon favorite among children around the world might have a little competition in the state of Tennessee. In 1978, the Tennessee Valley Railroad Museum was named the state's official railroad museum. In case you're interested in planning a visit, the museum's main terminal, Grand Junction Station, is located on Cromwell Road, just off Highway 153. You can find station number two, the East Chattanooga Depot, at 2202 North Chamberlain Avenue. Just don't plan on touring the railroad—the Chattanooga Depot is primarily a restoration area.

DID YOU KNOW?

Immortalized in the 1941 song, the "Chattanooga Choo Choo" is not actually a song about train. However, the city's locomotive legacy has been assured by the Chattanooga Choo Choo Hotel, where guests can stay the night in a restored railroad car.

Double Honors

There are two types of stone that have received special status in Tennessee over the years. On March 5, 1969, agate was recognized as the state's official stone. Ten years later, the state legislature also chose an official state rock. While agate is found naturally in just a few locations across the state, you can find limestone in just about every corner of the state. Limestone was named Tennessee's official state rock on February 28, 1979.

 If you happen to come across someone claiming that the official stone of Tennessee is Tennessee marble, you should probably hold your tongue rather than arguing with them. You may be surprised to learn that Tennessee marble is nothing more than a prettified version of limestone.

Rich in History

Knoxville's historic Tennessee Theatre has a long and rich history, dating back to November 1927, when Chicago contractor George M. Fuller first broke ground. On October 1, 1928, actress Clara Bow and her co-star James Hall starred in *The Fleet's In*, the first movie ever shown at the Tennessee Theatre.

One of the most notable features of the theatre is its legendary Wurlitzer pipe organ. Known as the "Mighty Wurlitzer," the organ has been a part of the theatre's tradition from the day it opened its doors. Aside from a 10-month period between October 2000 and August 2001—when the organ was shipped to Reno, Nevada, for repairs—it has been a constant part of the Tennessee Theatre.

LIVING (OR PREVIOUSLY LIVING) STATE SYMBOLS

Wooden Wonder

The fact that it grows in almost every corner of the state is one good reason why the tulip poplar (*Liriodendron tulipifera*) was designated Tennessee's official state tree. Because of its wide availability, the tulip poplar was the common wood used by pioneers looking to settle in the state to build their homes.

Aside from the practicality of the tulip tree, it's also one of the most beautiful trees in Tennessee, with greeny-orange, tulip-like flowers.

The yellowwood tree (*Cladrastis lutea*) was named the state's bicentennial tree in 1991.

Slippery Salute

In 1995, the General Assembly named the Tennessee cave salamander (*Gyrinophilus palleucus*) as the state's official amphibian. The snake-like, pinkish salamander ranges in size from only an inch or two in length to an almost frightening four feet long. This salamander is endemic to the U.S. and likes to live in karsts and caves.

In fact, these creatures are so shy that some colonies of Tennessee cave salamanders have been discovered 1200 feet inside caves submerged under 60 feet of water. Their lifespan is just as wide-ranging as their size and living habits, most living an average of 10 to 15 years, but some living until they're 25.

What's Under that Shell?

The eastern box turtle (*Terrapene carolina*) is a small, calm, little creature, measuring barely six inches long during adulthood. The box turtle's shell is spotted with yellow, orange and red flecks, and the little critter can live to the ripe old age of 60, though it rarely ventures very far from the place it was born. In 1995, the 99th General Assembly named the eastern box turtle the official state turtle.

Winged Creatures

The state of Tennessee has two official state insects, both named to the honor in 1975. The small, inconspicuous ladybug (*Coccinella septempunctata*) was recognized for its assistance to Tennessean farmers as a voracious devourer of insect pests. The firefly, or lightning bug beetle (*Photinus pyralis*), is a familiar flash of light on a dark Tennessee evening. Together, both bugs were perfect candidates for the honor, and really, who could ever choose between what are essentially two childhood favorites?

Buzzy as a Bee

The lovely little honeybee (*Apis mellifera*) doesn't just ensure flowers are pollinated from year to year—in the state of Tennessee, this industrious insect puts more than $119 million annually into the state coffers. In 1990, the honeybee's efforts were duly recognized when the state legislature named it the official agricultural insect of Tennessee.

Tone-on-Tone Beauty

The zebra swallowtail (*Eurytides marcellus*) is a striking creature with black and white stripes broken only by the red and blue spots on its lower back. This butterfly is found throughout most of the U.S., but in 1995, the 99th General Assembly named it Tennessee's official butterfly.

A Horse like None Other

According to the Tennessee Walking Horse Breeders' and Exhibitors' Association, the Narragansett Pacer, the Canadian Pacer, the Thoroughbred, the American Saddlebred and Standardbred stock have all contributed to breeding the official state horse. The Tennessee Walking Horse, also known as the "world's greatest show, trail and pleasure horse," was bestowed this honor in 2000.

Birds of a Feather

Tennessee officially recognizes two birds as state symbols.

The northern mockingbird (*Mimus polyglottos*) is a creature of simple beauty. Measuring about 10 inches from the tip of its head to the tip of its tail, the mockingbird is typically ashen gray in color with darker shades of gray on the wings, mixed with flecks of white on the wings and underbelly. While it doesn't sport any flamboyant colors, what sets the mockingbird apart is its distinctive call. Not only does it have its own unique song, but it's also known for mimicking the calls of other birds as well as the sounds of insects and amphibians. The mockingbird was named the official state bird in 1933.

Remember the swift-footed, cunning Road Runner? Well, he's got nothing on the bobwhite quail (*Colinus virginianus*) as far as small game sports fans are concerned. While it might not be the fastest bird out there, any avid hunter will tell you that the bobwhite quail, also known as the partridge, is "one of the finest game birds in the world." This relatively small, squat, little bird measures somewhere between eight and 10 inches in length and is mostly brown in color. It's also one of the most prolific egg layers, with females producing as many as 20 eggs in a clutch. In 1987, the Tennessee legislature named the bobwhite quail the state's official game bird.

WELCOME TO TENNESSEE

Here, Fishy, Fishy, Fishy

Folks in Tennessee are serious about their sport fishing, and their preferred catch of the day is always the largemouth bass (*Micropterus salmoides*). A good-sized largemouth, or "bigmouth" as it's also known, measures about 15 inches in length. By the time it gets to that size, the finned fellow is probably about three years old. In 1987, the largemouth bass was named the state's official sport fish.

But Tennesseans believe in doing things in a big way, and one special fish certainly isn't enough—even for a landlocked, farm-focused state like Tennessee. After all, there's such a thing as fish farms, and the Volunteer State is full of them, the majority of them farming channel catfish (*Ictalurus lacustris*), also known as "spotted cat" or "fiddler fish." Sport fishermen pull in most of these bottom-feeding specimens, and some of these monsters have weighed in at more than 60 pounds. The channel catfish was named the state's official commercial fish in 1987.

In Full Bloom

Avid nature lovers will know that Tennessee is renowned for its wide variety of wildflowers, and one of its loveliest blooms is the passionflower (*Passiflora incarnata*). The light purple blossom also goes by the names maypop, wild apricot and ocoee, and it is found throughout the southern United States. It was first singled out by the state's schoolchildren as a special flower in 1919, and, agreeing that Tennessee's youngsters made a valid point in extolling the passionflower's virtues, Senate Joint Resolution No. 13 recognized it as Tennessee's state flower.

In 1933, the iris (*Iridaceae*) started growing in popularity with garden enthusiasts across the state. In fact, it was so popular that the members of garden clubs across the state banded together and addressed state officials, claiming that the passionflower had never been "officially" adopted as the state flower. In 1933, iris lovers across Tennessee won their botanical battle, and the iris was granted status as the official state flower.

But that was not the end of the battle. The passionflower had its own fervent supporters, and they persisted in touting the merits of the original designation. And so, in 1973, the good folks at the Tennessee state legislature, who were by now more than likely just tired of listening to the argument, ended the feud once and for all and declared the passionflower to be the state's official wildflower, while the iris became the state's official cultivated flower.

Fantastic Fruit
It's a must in most kitchens and a favorite for any pasta lover. The tomato was recognized as Tennessee's official state fruit in 2003, even though most people think it's a vegetable.

Wild About Animals

The bushy, ring-tailed, black-masked raccoon lurks around most corners in Tennessee. Adult 'coons can weigh between 12 and 25 pounds and feed on frogs and fish. This cute little critter was named Tennessee's official wild animal in 1971.

Andrew Jackson was a much-loved president with more than a few nicknames to his credit. During the Creek War of 1813–14, he earned the name "Old Hickory" because his resolve was as strong as hickory—nothing could stop him. He was also called the "Hero of New Orleans," recognizing his contributions in the War of 1812. Another moniker, "King Andrew the First," carried undertones of criticism with it—his critics thought he abused the title of president to pass some of his pet programs. He was also known as "Mischievous Andy," and the Creek Indians dubbed him "Sharp Knife Given."

WELCOME TO TENNESSEE

TENNESSEE AT A GLANCE

The state of Tennessee is complex and contradictory. Its lowlands to the west oppose its mountains in the east. Its culture is as much 21st-century innovation and progress as it is 19th-century Southern tradition and legacy. It is a state with a large rural population, punctuated by vibrant, growing, diverse urban centers. Out of all of these clashing forces, a dynamic culture, economy and population has emerged.

Population at a Glance

According to estimates from the U.S. Census Bureau:

☛ Tennessee has an average of 138 people per square mile, based on 2000 population estimates of 5,689,270.

☛ Also in 2000, there were an estimated 2,232,905 households in the state with an average of 2.5 persons per household.

WELCOME TO TENNESSEE

- Tennessee welcomed 59,385 residents from other countries between 2000 and 2005.

- From 2006 estimates, the state's population had increased by 349,541, or 6.1 percent, to approximately 6,038,811 citizens.

- Tennessee's median household income in 2007 was $42,389.

- In 2007, it was estimated that 15.8 percent of Tennessee's population lived below the poverty line.

- By 2008, Tennessee had a population of about 6,214,888, making it the 19th most populated state in the United States.

- About 1,149,693 persons aged five years and older in the state are living with a disability.

- There are more females in Tennessee than males—women make up 51.3 percent of the state's population.

- Tennessee is full of babies, as 6.7 percent of the state's population is under five years old.

- Tennessee is also full of teenagers, as 24.6 percent of the population is younger than 18.

- There are lots of grandmas and grandpas, too—12.4 percent of Tennesseans are 65 or older.

- About 75.9 percent of the population has graduated from high school, which is lower than the national average of 80.4 percent.

- Approximately 19.6 percent of the population has a bachelor's degree or higher, which also falls under the national average of 24.4 percent.

- Metropolitan Nashville is one of the fastest growing urban areas in America.

WELCOME TO TENNESSEE

☞ Many new residents from California, Florida and some northern states are attracted by Tennessee's low cost of living and the healthcare and automobile industries that have blossomed in Nashville and around the rest of the state.

 About 20 percent of Tennessee's population declare that they were born "outside the South."

Tennessee Population Through the Years

Census year	Population
1790	35,691
1800	105,602
1850	1,002,717
1900	2,020,616
1950	3,291,718
2000	5,689,283

Roots in the Past

According to the analysis of U.S. Census figures from 2000, about 60 percent of Tennessee's residents named at least one ancestry: 17.3 percent of respondents claimed American heritage, 13 percent said they were of African American origin, 9.3 percent were Irish, 9.1 percent were English and 8.3 percent were German.

Ethnic Diversity

According to 2008 census estimates:

☞ 80.4 percent of the population is white, with 77.1 percent having no Hispanic origin, while the other 3.7 percent are of Hispanic or Latino origin.

- 16.8 percent of the population is African American.
- 0.3 percent of the population is American Indian or Alaskan Native.
- 1.3 percent of the population is Asian.
- 0.1 percent of the population is Native Hawaiian or other Pacific Islander.

(Note: The "Hispanic or Latino" category can include people of any race, which is why the figures listed don't always add up to 100 percent.)

The largest 10-year jump in the state's population in terms of a percentage increase was between 1790 and 1800—the 69,911-person increase represented a 195.9-percent population explosion.

Worship Preferences

About 82 percent of the state's population claims to be Christians, and more than 40 percent of those Christians claim to adhere to the tenets of the Baptist Church. Less than 10 percent of the state's residents claim they don't follow any faith practice. There is only one percent of the population that claims to follow the tenets of Islam, and 0.5 percent follow Judaism.

Naming a New Generation

In 2007, the Division of Health Statistics reported the top-10 most popular baby names for boy and girls born in Tennessee:

Girls	Boys
Madison	William
Emma	Jacob
Emily	Ethan
Addison	James

WELCOME TO TENNESSEE

Abigail	Joshua
Hannah	Christopher
Ava	Jackson
Chloe	Michael
Isabella	Noah
Anna	John

 Using statistics obtained from an unnamed Columbia University economist, the *Memphis Flyer* reported that in July 2007, the average life expectancy in Tennessee was 75.2 years. The news source also noted that more than half the state's population had a body-mass index of more than 25—in other words, they were technically overweight or obese.

Native Land

Tennessee is no longer home to any federally recognized Native American tribes, but in the land's earliest history, there were six tribes who recognized the area as their tribal lands.

The Cherokee tribes ran north and south and were nestled along the eastern portion of the state.

The Yuchi's traditional areas bordered that of the Cherokee with one exception: the Koasati tribal lands occupied the southern border of the Yuchi tribal lands and the northern border of Alabama. It's believed that the Yuchi language isn't related to any other language known today.

The Shawnee traditionally occupied a pie-shaped section of what later became Tennessee, bordering the state's northern limits, with the Yuchi to the east and the Chickasaw to the west.

The Chickasaw traditionally occupied a significant portion of western Tennessee with one exception: the state's southwestern corners—that portion belonged to the Quapaw tribe.

Most Populous Cities

Including its catchment area, the city of Nashville—Tennessee's capital city—is about 552,120 strong. But this big city isn't the largest in the state. That honor belongs to Memphis, with a population of 670,902. The eight cities that follow round out the top-10 most populated cities in the state:

Knoxville	182,337
Chattanooga	155,190
Clarksville	113,175
Murfreesboro	92,559
Jackson	62,711
Johnson City	59,866
Franklin	55,870
Kingsport	44,191

Making Sense of Dollars in the Volunteer State

Tennessee reported a Gross State Product (GSP) of $252,127 billion in 2008. This ranked the state as having the 19th largest economy in America. In 2007, the personal income per capita in Tennessee was $33,373. This number represents a rise of 17 percent since 2004.

Major economic outputs in the state include textiles, cotton, electrical power and cattle—59 percent of Tennessee's 82,000 farms are dedicated to raising cattle. Cotton farming is mostly relegated to the southwest corner of the state, where the upper portion of the Mississippi Delta's fertile soil stretches into the state.

Many large corporations have their headquarters in Tennessee, including the FedEx Corporation, AutoZone Incorporated and International Paper, which are all based in Memphis. Pilot

Corporation and Regal Entertainment Group call Knoxville home, while Eastman Chemical Company is based in Kingsport. Nissan's North American headquarters is based in Franklin, just south of Nashville, and Caterpillar Financial is located in Music City. Nissan also has a large manufacturing facility located in Smyrna.

Tennessee does not have a state income tax, so most of the state's income is based on a system of sales tax. Most items are subject to a seven percent tax, while food is regulated at 5.5 percent. However, candy and prepared foods are charged the full seven percent. Local sales taxes are also levied against consumer goods. Generally, the sales tax in Tennessee can run from 8.5 percent to as high as 9.75 percent, one of the highest rates in the country.

On the Move in Tennessee

Tennessee is definitely a car-driving state. Although urban centers have public transit, the systems are limited compared to what one would find in most other cities in the country. Most Tennesseans travel from point A to point B utilizing the Interstate highway system that connects the state from east to west and north to south. Interstate 40—and its various branches: I-240, I-440, I-140 and 1-640—links the state from east to west, while the I-55, I-65, I-75 and I-81 run from north to south. The I-26 links Kingsport to the North Carolina border near Johnson City, while the I-24 connects Chattanooga to Clarksville.

Tennessee is also home to a number of airports. Both Nashville (BNA) and Memphis (MEM) boast international airports. Other localities with airports include: Knoxville (McGhee Tyson Airport), Chattanooga (Chattanooga Metropolitan

Airport) and Jackson (McKellar-Sipes Regional Airport). The Tri-Cities Regional Airport is located near Blountville.

Tennessee is also served by Amtrak's City of New Orleans line, which services both Newbern and Memphis. The line runs from Louisiana to Illinois.

DID YOU KNOW?

Memphis International Airport serves as the major hub for the FedEx Corporation, which is the largest air-cargo operation in the world.

The Law of the Land

Tennessee's law and governmental structure is similar to that of most states, but, again like most states, Tennessee has its own particular way of conducting the business of the state.

- ☛ Tennessee's governor has a four-year term. Two consecutive terms is the maximum length of service as governor. The only official who is elected in a statewide contest is the governor. The Tennessee Senate elects a speaker who also serves as lieutenant governor.

- ☛ The Tennessee General Assembly consists of 33 state senators and 99 representatives. Senators serve for four years, while representatives serve for two. The Senate and the House each elect their own speakers.

- ☛ The Tennessee Supreme Court is the highest legal authority in the state. The Supreme Court is made up of one chief justice and four associate justices. The attorney general is appointed by the Supreme Court. Tennessee is the only state that does this.

☞ The Tennessee State Constitution was adopted in 1870. It was preceded by two earlier constitutions. Martial law is outlawed within the state. This may be because of Tennessee's occupation by Union troops during the Civil War.

Tennessee Plays Politics

When it comes to presidential elections, Tennessee went to Dwight D. Eisenhower twice in the '50s and has continued to lean toward the Republican Party ever since. That being said, it is also understood that Tennessee is more moderately conservative than her neighboring states, especially those of the Deep South. Republicans dominate East Tennessee, while Democrats pick up nearly half of the state's electorate in Middle and West Tennessee, where urban and African American populations in Nashville, Memphis and elsewhere follow national trends, skewing Democratic. In 2000, former U.S. senator and vice president from Tennessee, Al Gore, couldn't carry the state against George W. Bush. Bush went on to increase his margin of victory in the state by 10 percent when he faced John Kerry in 2004.

Tennessee appoints nine members to the U.S. House of Representatives, along with its two senators. In 2008, the Republicans won both houses of the legislature for the first time since the end of the Civil War. The state also went "red" for the defeated presidential candidate John McCain that same year.

DID YOU  KNOW?

Tennessee's 1st congressional district has been in the Republican camp since 1881. The 2nd congressional district has been with the party since 1873!

Enforcing the Law

Tennessee has four agencies that enforce the laws of the state:

- Tennessee Highway Patrol
- Tennessee Wildlife Resources Agency
- Tennessee Bureau of Investigation
- Tennessee State Parks Department

WELCOME TO TENNESSEE

THE FOUNDING OF TENNESSEE

The story of the founding of the Volunteer State is fraught with pride, prejudice, tragedy and triumph. It is a story of adventure and bravery, but also one about war and racism. The first Tennesseans were resourceful, resilient individuals who pushed their way into the Southern wilderness and helped found an important part of America's burgeoning national identity. Along the way, they cut the paths that lead to everything from the Trail of Tears to Dolly Parton, from the Memphis barbecue to the atomic bomb.

Of Kings

- In 1606, King James I charters the region that comprises modern-day Tennessee as a British province.

- In 1672, King James II gifts the entire region—from the Appalachians to the Pacific Ocean—to eight of his friends. The vast acreage is chartered as "The British Province of Carolina." At 150,000 square miles, the gift is so expansive that there is no way for the lucky recipients to fully comprehend the breadth of the king's generosity.

- In 1693, these friends of the king decide to separate the region into equal parts. A British lieutenant named Henry Timberlake makes the first visit to the Cherokee tribe that occupies the region. After establishing trust with the tribe, Timberlake creates the first crude maps of the region.

- In the mid 1700s, various factions vie for control of the territory west of the Appalachians. The southeastern Native tribes begin to push back against the British at the same time that colonists from the east begin to push down into the territories, seeking an alternative to the growing feudalism in the northeast.

Of Explorers

☛ In 1752, Daniel Boone follows an old Native American trading trail, crossing the then-unnamed Cumberland Gap and finding a successful path through the mountains. Boone develops the trail, providing passage for more settlers.

☛ In 1796, William Bean crosses the Appalachians solo and begins a new settlement near the Watauga River.

☛ James Robertson leads his family and another group over the mountains, but they become hopelessly lost. Robertson pushes on, ultimately abandoning his horse and passing out before he is found by local hunters, who lead him and his party to Bean's settlement. This is the beginning of Robertson's legend as a persevering leader. In the next few years, more of Tennessee's founding families arrived.

WELCOME TO TENNESSEE

Of Politicians

☛ Outside the legal reach of North Carolina, the growing group of settlers begins to govern themselves. The Articles of the Watauga Association create the first non-European civil government in American history.

☛ With the Revolutionary War on the horizon, the Watauga Association seeks tighter bonds with the North Carolina regional government in order to support the war effort. The British respond by arming Cherokee and Creek tribes, who begin a bloody war with the Tennessee woodsmen.

☛ Facing pressure from the tribes and abandoned by the North Carolina government, James Robertson and John Donelson lead two groups of settlers away from the Watauga community toward the Cumberland River. The first cabins on the bluff overlooking the Big Salt Lick River are the very beginnings of the city of Nashville.

WELCOME TO TENNESSEE

- In 1780, 256 men convene at Fort Nashborough to ratify the Cumberland Compact. After the Revolutionary War, the group presses for their own independence, creating the state of Franklin. They choose the name of Benjamin Franklin in the hope that he would support their claim to independent statehood.

- For years, "Franklinites" skirmish with North Carolina loyalists—sometimes violently—as each tries to lay claim to the governorship of the territory. The Continental Congress vows a hands-off policy, letting the settlers decide their own fate.

- In 1789, the North Carolina government relinquishes control of the area. They repay many of their Revolutionary War soldiers—including Franklinite loyalists—with large tracts of land and give control of the territory back to the federal government.

- The U.S. Government creates boundaries for the territory and appoints William Blount as governor. Blount creates his regional government at the site of Knoxville.

- In 1793, Blount leverages the territory's exploding population into a bid for statehood.

- In 1796, President George Washington signs Tennessee's statehood proclamation, making the region one of the very first territories to become a state.

The first two men from Tennessee to serve as U.S. state senators were William Blount and William Cocke—both men were named to the position in 1796.

WELCOME TO TENNESSEE

FOUNDING FATHERS AND HISTORIC HEROES

John Sevier

Soldier, statesman and pioneer, John Sevier was married at the age of 16 and was at the vanguard of the Tennessee frontier from his teenage years until he was elected the state's first governor in 1796. Sevier was born in New Market, Virginia, in 1745. He was the oldest of seven children born to prosperous farmers. After his marriage in 1761, he made a living as a farmer, a fur dealer, land speculator and tavern owner. In 1776, he moved his family to the Watagua River settlement, in what would later become Tennessee. Sevier became a representative of the Washington District of North Carolina and was dispatched to the Provincial Congress of North Carolina. Sevier was made a lieutenant-colonel of North Carolina during the Revolutionary War, gaining a reputation as a military man at the Battle of Kings Mountain in 1780, where his frontier troops clashed with the Tories and British soldiers near Spartanburg, South Carolina. In 1785, after the war, Sevier became the only governor of the unsuccessful state of Franklin. He was a colorful character who is best describing in an inscription on a monument in Knoxville:

> *John Sevier, pioneer, soldier, statesman, and one of the founders of the Republic; Governor of the State of Franklin; six times Governor of Tennessee; four times elected to Congress; a typical pioneer, who conquered the wilderness and fashioned the State; a protector and hero of Kings Mountain; fought thirty-five battles, won thirty-five victories; his Indian war cry, 'Here they are! Come on boys!'*

James Robertson

Born in 1742, in Brunswick County, Virginia, James Robertson was a striking man with a six-foot frame and piercing blue eyes. He was known for his even-tempered nature, a quality that served him well in dangerous, stressful circumstances, enabling him to become a leader, a hero and the "Father of Middle Tennessee." In 1769, while bringing his family across the Appalachians to the Watauga River settlement, Robertson famously got quite lost. However, his unflagging perseverance ensured his party's survival. In 1772, Robertson was elected as a magistrate of the Watauga Association. In 1779, he led a party from the Watauga settlement to a new location near the Cumberland River, where he eventually established Fort Nashborough. The fort was repeatedly attacked by Cherokee forces for several years, and Robertson lost two brothers, two sons and was shot three times as a result of the brutal fighting. As usual, Robertson persevered and encouraged those around him to do the same. Eventually, the Cherokee attacks ended and the community that would one day become Nashville began to thrive.

DID YOU KNOW?

James Robertson was appointed the post of brigadier general of the U.S. Army of the Territory South of the River Ohio by President George Washington.

Andrew Jackson

A controversial and contradictory figure, the legend of Andrew Jackson looms large in American history and in the state of Tennessee. Jackson was born in South Carolina in 1767. While still a young man, he volunteered for service during the Revolutionary War and ended up as a prisoner of war for a time. He finished his education after the war, moving to

North Carolina in 1784 and receiving his law degree in 1787. Within a year, he was appointed district attorney in Mero District (now Middle Tennessee) and moved to Nashville, where he met and married Rachel Donelson, the daughter of John Donelson, with whom he raised a number of Native American orphans.

In 1797, Jackson became a U.S. senator, though he resigned in 1798 to become a judge of the Superior Court (now the Tennessee Supreme Court). In 1802, he was elected major general of the Tennessee militia, a post he served for 20 years. He won national honor, but his fame was tarnished by political and personal controversy. In 1803, Jackson nearly fought a deadly duel with Tennessee governor John Sevier. In 1806, he dueled Charles Dickinson and shot him dead. In 1807, he ran a sword through Samuel Jackson, and he brawled with Jesse and Thomas Hart Benton in 1813, taking a bullet in the arm. Jackson's distinguished service in the War of 1812 won him national attention. Jackson controversially disobeyed orders when he was told to abandon his men, earning the nickname "Old Hickory" for his stubbornness. His defeat of British forces in New Orleans in 1815 made him a military legend, second only to George Washington himself.

During this time, Jackson negotiated land cessions all over the Southeast with the Cherokees, Choctaws and Chickasaws, foreshadowing his controversial presidential policy of the removal of Native tribes from these lands. This policy resulted in the tragic Trail of Tears, which was the forcible relocation of Native Americans in the Southeast to newly established Indian Territories in Oklahoma. Hunger, disease and exhaustion along the forced march resulted in the deaths of over 4000 Cherokee tribespeople. Andrew Jackson was elected president of the United States in 1828 and served two terms before retiring to his home, known as the Hermitage, in Nashville.

DID YOU  KNOW?

Andrew Jackson is buried in the garden at the Hermitage.

John Donelson

A land speculator and early settler of Middle Tennessee, John Donelson earned his place in Tennessee history after leading a party of more than 100 settlers on a grueling journey to the future Fort Nashborough settlement on the Cumberland River. While James Robertson led his group overland from the Watauga settlement, Donelson's fragile fleet of 30 canoes, flatboats and dugouts navigated a path through the Holston, Tennessee, Ohio and Cumberland rivers. Donelson kept a record of the journey in his diary, inscribing it as the "Journal of a Voyage, intended by God's permission, in the good boat *Adventure*, from Fort Patrick Henry, on Holston River, to the French Salt Springs, on Cumberland River." He filled the book with horrific accounts of what the group was forced to endure along the way, including attacks by Native tribes, hunger, exhaustion, a smallpox outbreak, extreme cold, treacherous shoals and swiftly moving currents. On April 24, 1780—after traveling nearly 1000 miles—the little group finally reached their destination. A week later, the Cumberland Compact was ratified. John Donelson was the fifth man to sign the document.

Sam Houston

Although Sam Houston is considered a hero in Texas, his career in Tennessee was also a colorful one. Houston was born in Virginia in 1793. A restless boy, he would often spend time with a nearby Cherokee tribe. The chief, Oolooteka, became a father figure to Houston and taught him the ways of the Cherokee. In 1813, Houston joined the army. He was badly wounded while fighting a tribe of Creeks at the Battle of Horseshoe Bend, but then-general Andrew Jackson noticed

his bravery and assigned him to a post near Nashville, where Houston became a part of the general's political machine. Sam Houston studied law in Nashville and opened a practice in Lebanon, Tennessee. He soon became the attorney general for Davidson County and went on to win an election to the U.S. House of Representatives before he became the governor of Tennessee in 1827.

David "Davy" Crockett

One of the most colorful characters in American history, David "Davy" Crockett's story is so much larger than life that it's difficult to tell where the man ends and the myth begins. A frontiersman as well as a Tennessee and United States congressman, Crockett quickly became a folk hero and a pop-culture legend as tales of his adventures and heroism spread across the country.

Crockett was born in 1786, in East Tennessee's Greene County. He spent all but the last few years of his life in the state, and he was at the forefront of the movement to push settlement from the Appalachians to the state's western border and on to Texas. An errant student, Crockett eventually ran away from home to escape from his father's wrathful fits. Returning home one year later, the young Crockett had grown so tall and so strong that his family didn't recognize him at first. The prodigal son found that his father's temper had greatly diminished in the shadow of Davy's new solid stature, and the two made peace.

Crockett was instrumental in the founding of Tennessee, teaming up with a number of loggers to widen and establish a permanent throughway at the Cumberland Gap, the passage through the lower Appalachians that made settling the Volunteer State possible. Crockett moved to Franklin County, where he twice volunteered as a soldier in the Indian Wars of 1813–15. He served as a justice of the peace and the town commissioner of Lawrenceberg, and he was a colonel in the militia before gaining a greater profile as a representative in the state legislature in 1821. Crockett became a U.S. congressman in 1827, campaigning as an honest man and an excellent marksman—a real "straight shooter." Re-elected for two additional terms, Crockett made a name for himself through his championing of homesteaders' rights to buy new properties at a low price. This was in direct opposition to Andrew Jackson, who sought to auction lands to the highest bidder to raise money for a state education program.

Meanwhile, Crockett's legend continued to grow. He was the subject of biographies, plays and numerous articles. In 1834, Crockett published his autobiography, *A Narrative of the Life of David Crockett of the State of Tennessee*, and he always displayed a sophisticated understanding of his personal image, which he often used for political advantage. In 1836, Crockett moved to Texas seeking new political possibilities and hoping to make his fortune as a land speculator, but it was not to be.

Within weeks of his arrival in Texas, General Antonio Lopez de Santa Anna laid siege to the Alamo. Numerous accounts speak to Crockett's leadership and bravery during the two-week struggle, and though no one knows for sure, it is thought that Crockett was among the handful of prisoners who were captured and executed after Santa Anna's troops overran the fort. The uncertainty surrounding his death fueled the legend of Davy Crockett and has insured his immortality to this day.

DID YOU  KNOW?

Actor Fess Parker played Davy Crockett in the 1950s television series, and John Wayne played the hero in *The Alamo*, a film that Wayne himself produced, directed and starred in.

Nathan Bedford Forrest

No other Civil War soldier from the Army of Tennessee spawned a legend that looms as large as that of Nathan Bedford Forrest.

Born in Chapel Hill, Tennessee, on July 13, 1821, Forrest took over as the head of his household at the age of 16 after the death of his father. Although Forrest possessed less than a year of formal education, his success in the slave trade saw him rise from a subsistence farmer to a wealthy planter, acquiring substantial properties along the way. After Tennessee seceded from the Union, Forrest, his youngest brother and his 15-year-old son all volunteered for service with the Seventh Tennessee Calvary. Governor Isham G. Harris authorized Forrest to raise a full regiment of mounted troops, and the newly appointed leader trained and armed the men largely at his own expense. In December 1861, at his first battle in Sacramento, Kentucky, Forrest demonstrated two traits that would make him a military legend: his common-sense tactics and his proficiency as a brutal close-combat soldier. At six-foot-two and over 200 pounds, Forrest was truly an imposing soldier. It is estimated that he killed more than 30 men in face-to-face combat, using pistols, shotguns and his famous, heavy saber sharpened on both the top and bottom edges. The brave soldier's career and future fame seemed to grow with every successful engagement.

In 1862, Forrest's decision to lead his men out of Fort Donelson rather than surrender won him accolades for his boldness, and he was promoted to colonel. His new position found him at Shiloh, where he was wounded during the retreat of the Confederate Army. After a courageous raid against a Union outpost in Murfreesboro, Forrest was promoted to brigadier-general later that year. While the Army of Tennessee suffered numerous defeats to Union forces, Forrest waged a successful campaign of raids all over West Tennessee, crippling railroad lines and destroying supply chains all over the region. On December 4, 1863, Forrest—now a major general—raided and captured Fort Pillow, just north of Memphis. When the fort's largely African American troops attempted to surrender, they were fired upon and more than half of the approximately 600 troops were killed in what became known as the "Fort Pillow Massacre."

Shortly after Fort Pillow, Forrest stopped a larger Union force at Brice's Cross Roads in Mississippi—this was seen as the general's greatest achievement. When the Army of Tennessee was making its last retreat from Nashville near the end of the war, it was Forrest's command of the rearguard that saved the force from total extermination.

After being promoted to lieutenant general in February 1865, Forrest surrendered his command at Gainesville, Alabama, in May of that same year. Following his service in the war, Forrest returned to Tennessee, but he wasn't happy just quietly retiring. By 1867, Forrest had joined the Ku Klux Klan and may have become its first Grand Wizard. During this time, the Klan was responsible for violence against African Americans and other whites who were fighting for the voting rights of blacks. Forrest was never directly tied to any specific KKK activities, and in his last public speech, he spoke of reconciliation between the races. His mixed legacy of heroism and racism makes the general one of the most controversial of all legendary Tennesseans to this day.

Other Notable Tennesseans

- Casey Jones was a real-life train engineer—born in Jackson, Tennessee—who risked his life and lost, in an effort to stop his train from colliding with a stalled freight train. Although he died, his heroic actions saved his passengers. The song "Casey Jones" was written in his honor.

- Sequoya was a Cherokee silversmith who developed the alphabet that would provide the Cherokee Nation with a means for a written language. He's considered the "only known man in the history of the world to single-handedly develop an alphabet."

WELCOME TO TENNESSEE

TENNESSEE AND THE CIVIL WAR

In 1861, the United States began to pull apart, and so did Tennessee. The state broke down along the borders of its three geographic regions: the West Tennessee region was compelled to pledge its loyalty to the Confederate States of America that was forming in Alabama; East Tennesseans were loyal to the Union; and citizens in Middle Tennessee saw entire communities fracturing along various fault lines, paving the way for vicious guerrilla warfare between families and neighbors once the war commenced.

To Secede or Not to Secede

- In 1861, Governor Isham G. Harris called a special session to consider secession. The legislature decided to put the matter in the hands of the people, scheduling a referendum vote in February. Voting 69,000 to 58,000, Tennesseans decided against holding a secession convention despite the fact that the Deep South was boiling over with secession fervor.

- The attack on Fort Sumter later that year and President Lincoln's call for 75,000 soldiers from the state militia to put down the Southern rebellion made many Tennesseans reconsider their loyalty to the Union, while others contemplated removing their individual counties from the state entirely if it sided with the Confederacy.

- In May 1861, Governor Harris and the legislature declared the state's independence amid these new doubts. This was followed by a new referendum vote in which 105,000 citizens favored secession, with less than half that number against it.

- Many of the counties in East Tennessee sought permission to form a separate state. A peaceful break was not in the offing, though, and the offending counties were soon occupied by troops loyal to the Confederacy.

- Later that summer, 31,000 soldiers rushed north from Tennessee to join up with Union forces in Kentucky. More Tennesseans volunteered to fight for the Union than from all the other Southern states combined, as per their reputation.

- In September 1861, General Albert Sidney Johnston took charge of the Tennessee forces and accelerated the construction of Fort Henry on the Tennessee River and Fort Donelson on the Cumberland River.

- On January 19, 1862, the Battle of Mill Springs near Somerset, Kentucky, ended when the Confederate forces of General George Crittenden and General Felix Zollicoffer were defeated by the Union troops of General George H. Thomas. As a result, Tennessee's eastern defenses were abandoned to shore up the war efforts in Middle Tennessee.

- By February 16, land and naval forces under the command of Ulysses S. Grant destroyed and overran both Fort Henry and Fort Donelson. By February 16, Tennessee's defensive line had completely collapsed and both the Tennessee River and the Cumberland River were under Union control.

- On February 23, Union troops entered Tennessee's capital, Nashville. This was the first state capital to fall in the Confederacy.

- On April 6, General Johnston attempted to take out Grant's forces before they recombined with another Union army. The troops clashed near Shiloh Church, initiating one of the bloodiest battles of the war. The rebel soldiers drove Grant back to the Tennessee River, but Grant rallied in the night and the Union forces won the day.

- By June 6, the Union forces had taken Memphis with a combined land and naval attack that caused the collapse of Tennessee's provisional government, which had been limping along since the evacuation of Nashville.

- Regrouping in Mississippi, the Army of Tennessee concocted a plan to take back their state and joined Kentucky in the Confederacy—however, after the battle of Perryville, the plan was abandoned in failure.

- In December, Nathan Bedford Forrest secured his legend as a cavalry genius and a heroic fighter by taking garrisons at Union City, Dyer and Trenton in West Tennessee.

- On December 31, during the battle of Stones River, Union forces repelled a rebel sneak attack south of Nashville.

- By September 1863, General Ambrose Burnside's Union forces had entered Knoxville, where they were greeted as liberating forces by throngs of East Tennesseans who had always been against secession.

- On September 19, Confederate forces clashed with Union soldiers south of Chattanooga in the Battle of Chickamauga. The Union forces were broken and retreated to Chattanooga, where General Bragg's rebel army laid siege to the city.

- Between November 23 and 25, General Grant sent reinforcements to Chattanooga and re-supplied the city. Shortly after Union forces took Lookout Mountain in the Battle Above the Clouds, Bragg's siege was shattered and his forces retreated into Georgia. An attempt to retake Knoxville fared even worse, with Union soldiers only suffering 13 casualties compared to 800 casualties inflicted on the attacking rebel forces. By the end of 1863, the entire state was technically under the control of the Union.

- During the last years of the Civil War, while under Union occupation, slavery came to an end in Tennessee. Former slaves were treated to food, clothing, medicine and shelter in refugee camps. Freed blacks were also hired to assist the Union Army with its mission. Over 2700 former slaves built Fort Negley in Nashville, and thousands of others were employed in Memphis. By 1863, former slaves who wanted to fight for the Union were allowed to join.

☛ After 1864 and until the end of the conflict, most of the action in the western Confederate states took place in Georgia. However, Tennesseans continued to suffer terrible hardships. Many small, mostly independent guerrilla bands continued to attack Union garrisons, destroying train lines, stealing supplies and capturing prisoners. Communities were terrorized by outlaw bands, murder and arson were commonplace and basic commodities for day-to-day living were very hard to come by.

☛ On November 30, 1864, after nearly trapping Union general John Schofield at Spring Hill, the Army of Tennessee troops attacked his entrenched forces. In the Battle of Franklin, the Army of Tennessee suffered terrible losses—6300 casualties, including 12 generals (six killed) and 54 regimental commanders.

☛ Schofield retreated to Nashville for the last major Civil War battle in the state. The Battle of Nashville began on December 15, 1864. Badly out-manned by the Union forces occupying Nashville, the Army of Tennessee was forced to retreat. Although skirmishes would continue until the end of the conflict, the Army of Tennessee was officially disbanded after the Battle of Nashville.

Of the 179,000 soldiers who fought in the American Civil War, approximately 60,000 were Tennesseans.

WELCOME TO TENNESSEE

GEOGRAPHY

How Big?

Tennessee measures 491 miles from east to west and 115 miles from north to south, equaling about 42,146 square miles. That makes it the 36th largest state in the United States.

Land vs. Water

Of Tennessee's total area, 41,200 square miles is land and 926 square miles is water.

Center Point

Log in a longitude of 86°37.3' W and a latitude of 35°47.7' N, and you'll find yourself about five miles northeast of the community of Murfreesboro in Rutherford County. In other words, you'll be at the geographical center of Tennessee.

DID YOU  KNOW?

Tennessee is made up of 11 physiographic provinces: the Mississippi Flood Plain, Coastal Plain, West Tennessee Uplands, Western Highland Rim, Central Basin, Eastern Highland Rim, Cumberland Plateau, Cumberland Mountains, Sequatchie Valley, Ridge and Valley and the Blue Ridge Mountains.

Next-Door Neighbors

Tennessee is bordered by eight states: Kentucky, Virginia, North Carolina, Georgia, Alabama, Mississippi, Arkansas and Missouri. The only other state with that many states bordering it is Missouri, which is also surrounded by eight states.

Triple Threat

Tennessee has three natural divisions. The eastern portion of the state is characterized by mountains, along with a generally rugged terrain. The Cumberland Plateau occupies a large portion of Middle Tennessee, and West Tennessee is mostly composed of the Gulf Coastal Plain. Together, these are commonly referred to as the three Grand Divisions.

Capital City

Nashville is the capital city of Tennessee—however, it hasn't always been that way. In fact, Tennessee has had four different cities serving in this capital capacity during its history: Knoxville, Kingston, Murfreesboro and Nashville. Nashville was the final choice for a permanent capital in 1843.

High Points

The picturesque Clingmans Dome, in the heart of the Great Smoky Mountains National Park, is notable for several reasons. At an elevation of 6643 feet, it's the highest point in Tennessee—it is also recognized as the second highest point east of the Mississippi, though it didn't lose by much. Mount Mitchell, in North Carolina, is the highest point by a mere 41 feet.

Middle Ground

Overall, Tennessee's average elevation is 900 feet above sea level.

Low Point

At 178 feet, the Mississippi River is the lowest part of the state.

DID YOU  KNOW?

Tennessee is listed in the *Guinness Book of Records* on account of its "Lost Sea" in Sweetwater. The underground lake is the largest of its kind in the country. There are also 3800 caves in the state, making it a true spelunker's paradise.

Major Rivers

There are five major rivers in Tennessee:

- The Tennessee River measures 652 miles long and has been known by over 41 different names—for example, the Callamaco River and the Cherokee River—before it was officially named the Tennessee River in 1931.

- The Mississippi River is 2350 miles long, making it the third longest river in North America. Aside from Tennessee, the Mississippi River runs through nine other states.

- The Cumberland River measures 687 miles long and runs at an elevation of 1155 feet.

- The Clinch River runs for about 300 miles and has two dams—the Norris Dam and the Melton Hill Dam.

- The 270-mile-long Duck River is the only river located entirely within the state of Tennessee. On May 15, 2001, the 37 miles of the Duck River that runs through Maury County was named a state scenic river.

Major Lakes

There are five major lakes in Tennessee:

- Kentucky Lake was created by the Tennessee Valley Authority (TVA) in the hope of controlling flood levels on the lower Ohio and Mississippi rivers. Construction began on the artificial lake on July 1, 1938, and water began flowing into the reservoir on August 30, 1944. With more than 2000 miles of shoreline and a length of 184 miles, Kentucky Lake is the largest artificial lake in the country.

- Norris Lake spills into five counties: Anderson, Campbell, Claiborne, Grainger and Union.

- Chickamauga Lake was another TVA project. The reservoir creating this lake began filling on January 15, 1940. According to its website, the lake has "810 miles of shoreline [and] has 35,400 square acres of surface area." It was named in honor of the Chickamauga Indian tribe.

- Cherokee Lake is stocked with a wide array of fish: striped bass, black bass, walleye, sauger, crappie, sunfish, white bass and catfish.

- Tims Ford Reservoir is located in south central Tennessee. It's fed by the Elk River and is regulated by the Tims Ford Dam, located 34 miles upstream.

Geological Disasters

The New Madrid Seismic Zone runs beneath the southern and midwestern United States. Tennessee is one of seven states in the country that is directly affected by earthquakes along that fault line, as was evidenced by the New Madrid earthquakes of 1811 and 1812. The most significant quakes during this period of geological occurrences resulted in toppled chimneys and severe landslides, and raised and sunk parts of the landscape.

There have been several powerful earthquakes in Tennessee over its history. According to the U.S. Geological Service, the following quakes were the most significant:

WELCOME TO TENNESSEE

- On January 4, 1843, a severe, intensity VIII earthquake hit Memphis and the western part of Tennessee. The shock was felt across one million square miles.

- The eastern portion of the state was hit by what was classified as a "strong shock" on March 28, 1913. The tremors were centered on Knoxville and covered approximately 2700 square miles.

- Tennessee and Arkansas were both shaken up by an earthquake that hit the Mississippi Valley region on May 7, 1927.

- On November 16, 1941, an earthquake centered near Covington sent shock waves as far away as Memphis, Pleasant Hill and Ripley.

- Most of Tennessee reported feeling an earthquake of intensity VI on July 16, 1952. That earthquake was centered in Dyersburg.

- In the early hours of the morning of January 25, 1955, an earthquake with an intensity VI occurred near the Arkansas border and created shock waves that were strong enough to break windows.

The next couple of years saw a rash of seismic events in Tennessee:

- March 29, 1955, near Finley.

- January 28, 1956, centered in Covington.

- September 7, 1956, two earthquakes—both intensity VI—shattered windows and broke dishes 8300 square miles around the Knoxville area.

- Knoxville was shaken up all over again on October 30, 1973, with several tremors measuring V and VI in intensity.

WELCOME TO TENNESSEE

WEATHER AND CLIMATE
Moderate to Fair

Tennessee's climate could be generally categorized as "moderate"—summers are warm to hot, but winters are mild. However, there are some fluctuations because of the state's varied landscape. The Gulf Coastal Plain, Central Basin and Sequatchie Valley have the longest growing seasons, largely because the weather is warmest there. Winter is rainy season in Tennessee, and like winter in more northern states, that rainy season can stretch into the spring.

Here are a few highlights:

- Perryville has recorded the highest temperature in Tennessee history and has done it twice! Perryville registered 113°F on July 29 and August 9, 1930.

- Mountain City is located in East Tennessee. On December 30, 1917, it recorded the state's lowest temperature at –32°F.

- On average, residents of Tennessee can expect a mean summer temperature of around 90°F. In the winter, average temperatures are cooler, hovering around 40°F.

- Tennessee typically receives about 50 inches of precipitation yearly.

- There are about 15 tornadoes reported every year in Tennessee, ranging in intensity from mild to severe.

- A sad chapter in Morgan County's history occurred on November 10, 2002. On that day, a vicious tornado ripped through the county, tearing trees out of the ground, tossing vehicles around like they were toy cars, demolishing at least 50 homes, killing seven people and wounding another 28 people in the community of Mossy Grove.

Because Tennessee isn't directly on the Atlantic Ocean, it's pretty safe from the threat and damage of hurricane season. What its location does do, however, is make it a prime draw for thunderstorms—Tennessee has about 50 of them every year.

WELCOME TO TENNESSEE

AMAZING ANIMALS
Big Game Animals

Tennessee's big game animals are the black bear, deer, elk, wild boar and turkey:

- Tennessee's black bear population is stable enough that, during hunting season, the legal harvest has been 370 since 1997. In 1982, the legal harvest was only 21.

- The most popular big game animal in Tennessee is the whitetail deer. But even though hunters covet the animal, the whitetail deer population has increased from about 2000 in the 1940s to about 900,000 in 2005.

- Elk were once abundant in Tennessee before hunting and habitat pressure from early settlers and explorers lead to their disappearance. For more than 150 years, there were no elk in Tennessee until the Tennessee Wildlife Resources Agency reintroduced elk to the state. From the late 1990s until December 2000, Tennessee's elk herd increased to a population of about 201. Today, there are more than 300 elk in the state.

- With young piglets being sexually mature by the age of eight months, it's easy to see why Tennessee has such a healthy wild boar population.

- The wild turkey is another big game species that was at threatened one point in Tennessee, but populations have been restored thanks to the Tennessee Wildlife Resources Agency.

WELCOME TO TENNESSEE

Small Game Animals

Hunters have a wide variety of small game animals to beat the bushes for in Tennessee:

- Ever heard the saying "to play 'possum"? The term refers to the common defense used by opossums when faced with a threat—they like to play dead.

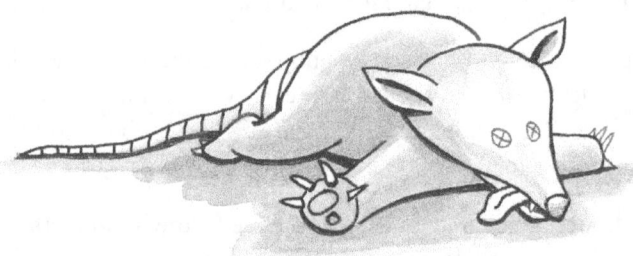

- Beavers are the largest rodents in North America and typically live between 10 and 20 years.

- Like the beaver, muskrats are also creatures of the water. However, they're considerably smaller, and hunters are only one threat to their safety—hawks, owls, raccoons, foxes, minks and even water snakes and large turtles are other natural predators of the muskrat.

- Bobcats are shy creatures, seldom coming into contact with humans. If you do happen to see one, they're immediately recognizable by their short, stubby tails and perky ears.

- The coyote is now common in Tennessee, but the state wasn't actually part of their original habitat. A greater numbers of coyotes—as well as two other small game species, the gray and red fox—moved into the area as the numbers of wolves declined, reducing their natural predators. However, encroaching development has lead to a decrease in available territory, and coyotes are now commonly spotted in urban centers like Nashville.

- Grouse and quail are popular birding options for small game hunters, though grouse are more common in Tennessee and the population of the bobwhite quail—Tennessee's official state bird—are steadily declining.

- Mink are tiny creatures, measuring between 19 and 36 inches from their nose to the tip of their eight-inch tails but weighing only between one and three pounds.

- According to the Tennessee Wildlife Resources Agency, the river otter is the "largest semi-aquatic predator found in Tennessee."

- At one time, eastern cottontail bunnies were found in abundance throughout the eastern half of the United States. But this bunny is very sensitive to changes in its environment and has suffered a decline in its population as a result of urban sprawl and other threats to its habitat.

- If you're into any kind of wilderness activities, it's quite possible that you'll stumble across a raccoon or two in your travels. The raccoon can be found throughout the state but is most apt to venture out under the cover of night.

- There are two kinds of skunks common in Tennessee: the striped skunk and the spotted skunk.

Birds of a Feather

There are three kinds of migratory birds that are hunted annually:

- The Tennessee Wildlife Resources Agency reports that there are about 100,000 mourning dove hunters in the state, and they "harvest an estimated two million or more doves annually."

- The waterfowl commonly hunted in Tennessee are ducks, coots, mergansers, gallinules, moorhens, Virginia rails, soras and Canadian geese.

- The woodcock is sometimes called the "timber-doodle" or just "doodle."

Bog Animals

Tennessee bogs are home to a wide variety of wildlife that is unique to the habitat. For example, the bog lemming (*Synaptomys cooperi*) thrives on the variety of grasses and sedges found in that environment. However, Tennessee bogs are rapidly becoming a shrinking wetland habitat and that means that several species of plants and wildlife, such as the bog turtle (*Clemmys muhlenbergii*), are finding themselves threatened—especially because the kind of bog they like best is found mostly on privately owned land. In some cases, a habitat that once covered almost 1000 acres of land has been reduced to a few dozen acres, and bog plants—like Tennessee's green pitcher plant and bog laurel—have been completely wiped out because of this land loss.

WELCOME TO TENNESSEE

AMPHIBIAN MANIA

It's All About the Frogs

Most folks associate frogs with the smooth-skinned *Anura*—amphibians without tails. Toads, on the other hand, often have rough, bumpy skin. Frogs usually live near water and can leap long distances, while toads, which aren't as slick and lean, take small hops and can be found quite a distance from water. However, the most interesting thing about toads is that they're still technically frogs despite their differences.

Either way, there are 21 species of frogs (and toads) in Tennessee. Here are some interesting facts about a few of them:

☛ The largest frog native to the U.S. is the American bullfrog (*Rana catesbeiana*). It takes up to five years for this species to reach maturity. The American bullfrog is common in "permanent" lakes or ponds throughout the state.

- The pickerel frog (*Rana palustris*) could easily have been called a leopard frog on account of its spotted body. This frog is not common in western Tennessee, but can be found most elsewhere.

- If you listen closely to a recording taped by Carl Gerhardt of the University of Missouri, the crawfish frog (*Rana areolata*) sounds like he's saying "waaaaaater" when he snores.

- The tadpoles of the green treefrog (*Hyla cinerea*) mature in just one or two months.

- A single barking treefrog (*Hyla gratiosa*) can deposit as many as 2000 eggs at one time.

- The bird-voiced treefrog (*Hyla avivoca*) doesn't croak at all. Its call sounds like a high-pitched, warbling birdsong.

- The spring peeper (*Pseudacris crucifer*) looks like a fall leaf and is known for the "X" markings on its back.

- The mountain chorus frog (*Pseudacris brachyphona*) is extremely small, reaching just 1.25 inches at maturity.

- There are several color variations of the northern cricket frog (*Acris crepitans*), but there's one thing they all have in common—a dark triangle between the eyes.

- The call of an American toad (*Bufo americanus*) is high-pitched and can last up to 30 seconds.

- A female Fowler's toad (*Anaxyrus fowleri*) can lay as many as 10,000 eggs at one time.

- When it's raining the hardest, the eastern spadefoot (*Scaphiopus holbrooki*) is most in the mood to create little spadefoots.

DID YOU KNOW?

The largest alligator snapping turtle *(Macrochelys temminckii)* in the world weighs 249 pounds and resides in the Tennessee

Aquarium. With a collection of 300 species of fish, birds, reptiles, amphibians and mammals—totaling over 7000 animals—the Tennessee Aquarium is the largest facility of its kind to focus on freshwater habitat.

Newts, Sirens, Amphiumas, Oh My!

More simply put, the animals mentioned in the title are all amphibians, and there are several different species that are common to Tennessee. These little creatures might look small and insignificant, but they're actually incredibly important for several reasons. They control the population of worms, snails and pesky insects, and they also provide food for other creatures. But most importantly, their skin is extremely sensitive to what's going on in their habitat, and scientists can use that to help identify any environmental problems.

These are just a few of the salamanders that are common to Tennessee:

- The southern two-lined salamander (*Eurycea cirrigera*) and the Blue Ridge two-lined salamander (*Eurycea wilderae*) are very similar in appearance, both measuring between 2.5 and 4.5 inches. The three-lined salamander (*Eurycea guttolineata*) is longer again, between four and seven inches in length.

- The lesser siren (*Siren intermedia*) stretches between seven and 27 inches at maturity.

- Measuring a slight 1.5 to two inches in length, the pygmy salamander (*Desmognathus wrighti*) is Tennessee's smallest salamander.

- The white-spotted slimy (*Plethodon cylindraceus*), northern slimy (*Plethodon glutinosus*) and Mississippi slimy (*Plethodon mississippi*) salamanders are all, well, slimy. At a typical length of between four and eight inches, they are all fairly large as far as salamanders go and have light-colored spots on their dark bodies.

WELCOME TO TENNESSEE

- The Tennessee cave salamander (*Gyrinophilus palleucus*) is considered one of the most unique salamanders in the state—it is lungless and instead breathes through its skin and special tissues in its mouth. It is found in only three states: Tennessee, Alabama and Georgia.

- Bet I don't have to tell you the easiest way to identify a four-toed salamander (*Hemidactylium scutatum*)? If you guessed that it has four toes on its hind legs, then you're right!

- The eastern red-backed (*Plethodon cinereus*) and southern red-backed (*Plethodon serratus*) salamanders were also once thought to be the same species, but they were later separated into two varieties after conducting a careful "biochemical analysis."

- The Jordan's (*Plethodon jordani*), red-legged (*Plethodon shermani*) and northern gray-cheeked (*Plethodon montanus*) are three different species of salamanders—however, they were once thought to be different races of the same species. All three are found along the state's eastern border, but each also inhabits distinct areas in the state: the Great Smoky Mountains National Park is home to the Jordan's salamander, the southeastern corner of Tennessee is the ideal habitat for the red-legged salamander and the northern gray-cheeked is found in the northeastern corner of the state.

- The northern dusky (*Desmognathus fuscus*), Santeetlah dusky (*Desmognathus santeetlah*) and spotted dusky (*Desmognathus conanti*) salamanders have several commonalities—they are all a light, dusky brown color and like to live in aquatic and semi-forested habitats.

- When the Yonahlossee salamander (*Plethodon yonahlossee*) reaches maturity, it sports a long, chestnut-colored patch from the back of its neck to the base of its tail.

- The stocky black-bellied salamander (*Desmognathus quadramaculatus*) has hardened toe tips that help it dig and climb, and it likes living in several different kinds of environments.

- Green salamanders (*Aneides aeneus*) aren't rare, but they are rarely seen. They like to live in places where they can blend in with their surroundings, like on rocks or on the bark of a fallen tree.

- The mud salamander (*Pseudotriton montanus*) and red salamander (*Pseudotriton ruber*) both have shorter tails than most other salamanders.

- At first glance, the eastern newt (*Notophthalmus viridescens*) is often thought to be a lizard, but don't tell him that.

- The eastern tiger salamander (*Ambystoma tigrinum*) looks more like a leopard, what with its many spots.

- The marbled salamander (*Ambystoma opacum*) is black with a silvery-white, diamond-studded pattern along its back and tail.

- While many salamanders have five toes, the Congo eel only has three—hence it's other name, the three-toed amphiuma.

- The mudpuppy, or waterdog (*Necturus maculosus*), loves the fast life—in other words, its favorite habitat is fast-flowing water and rocky-bottomed streams. This salamander is found in most of the state except for the northwesterly corner.

- The spring salamander (*Gyrinophilus porphyriticus*) is a predator that has been known to eat other salamanders and, aside from a single sighting in West Tennessee, this species is also found mostly in the eastern portion of the state, maybe because there are so many other salamanders to eat there.

- Because the Junaluska salamander (*Eurycea junaluska*) is so uncommon, even in its natural habitats, it is listed as "In Need of Management." Other salamanders "In Need of Management" in Tennessee are the Tellico (*Plethodon aureolus*), Weller's

(*Plethodon welleri*), Wehrle's (*Plethodon wehrlei*), mountain dusky (*Desmognathus ochrophaeus*), seepage (*Desmognathus aeneus*) and the Cumberland Plateau (*Plethodon kentucki*) salamanders.

Tennessee's largest species of salamander is the hellbender (*Cryptobranchus alleganiensis*), which measures between 12 and 29 inches in length. The hellbender used to be quite populous throughout the state, but recently, their numbers have declined drastically and this species is now listed as "In Need of Management."

WOODEN WONDERS

Champion Trees

Tennessee is home to 263 species of trees. In order to identify some of the larger species of trees native to the state, Tennessee developed a "Champion Tree Program," which was initiated in the mid 1970s.

Specimens in the Champion Tree Program are awarded points based on factors such as height, the spread of its crown and the circumference of its trunk. The tree earning the highest number of points in its species is then named a Champion Tree. Residents interested in the program usually collect this arboreal information and submit a tree and its location to the program, and officials visit that tree and judge whether or not it meets the criteria to be named a new Champion Tree. In 2002, the Champion Tree that had garnered the most points was the cherrybark oak, with a score of 485. The Tennessee Champion Tree with the fewest points at that time was the common prickly ash, with only 17 points.

Biggest and Best

In 2002, a government of Tennessee fact sheet named the northern red oak as Tennessee's largest tree, towering a full 172 feet. More recently, the Forest Resources Research and Education Center in Oak Ridge named a Shumard oak in Overton Park as the state's tallest tree—it measured 190 feet in 2009.

Home-Grown Biggie
The largest Champion tree located at the Tennessee Arboretum is the European black alder. It stands 55 feet in height and is located in the marsh area.

Short Stuff!
Measuring only nine feet in height, Tennessee's shortest champion is the Japanese yew.

Counts from the Counties

Forty-four of Tennessee's 94 countries are home to Champion Trees. When it comes to numbers, Knox County leads the pack with 32 Champion Trees, Fayette and Giles counties are tied with 26 champions, Shelby County has 25, Davidson County has 17 and there are 13 in Sevier County.

Hosts with the Most

The Great Smoky Mountains National Park is the single "owner" or location with the most Champion Trees—there are 25 different champion species in the park. The University of Tennessee is home to 16 species, while Meeman-Shelby State Park is home to 11.

WELCOME TO TENNESSEE

MOUNTAIN BOGS

The wet and marshy ecosystems known as mountain bogs are found throughout Tennessee. They vary in size from small wet areas easily distinguished by the naked eye to patches of land that extend for several hundred acres, and they provide scientists with a great way to study the evolution of the land and its plant life.

Rare Finds

Tennessee's mountain bogs are the perfect habitat for 36 species of rare or unique plants. Here are just a few of the more intriguing species:

- Cinnamon fern: a large species of fern found throughout most of Tennessee, with the exception of the counties along the state's western border.

- Royal fern: also found throughout most of the state, but prefers to grow in areas with partial sun or full shade.

- Wild azalea: common in Tennessee and one of 15 azalea species found throughout the eastern portion of the country.

- Golden club: a member of the arum family, it sports yellow spikes and grows to about 18 inches in height.

- Cranberry: Johnson County's Shady Valley is home to the Orchard Bog Preserve, a site that protects rare species like the wild cranberry and the bog turtle.

- Orchid: as many as 30 species of orchid have been identified as native to Tennessee.

- Bulrush: the California bulrush is only native or naturalized in two Tennessee counties: Obion and Rhea.

- Sundew: Tennessee is home to four different sundew species—red sundew (*Drosera brevifolia Pursh*), pink sundew (*Drosera capillaris Poir*), spoonleaf sundew (*Drosera intermedia Hayne*) and round-leaved sundew (*Drosera rotundifolia L.*)—all listed as threatened species in the state.

☛ Pitcher plants: these carnivorous plants love to eat crawling or flying insects.

Losing Ground

There are several mammals and reptiles that were once common to Tennessee that are now ranked as "S1," or "extremely rare and critically imperiled." They are the northern flying squirrel (*Glaucomys sabrinus*), the Indiana bat (*Myotis sodalis*), Kirtland's snake (*Clonophis kirtlandii*), the bog turtle (*Clemmys muhlenbergii*) and the coal skink (*Eumeces anthracinus*).

WELCOME TO TENNESSEE

SPIRITUAL STATE: RELIGION IN TENNESSEE

Religious Rankings

In 2010, a new report issued by the Pew Forum on Religion & Public Life ranked what they had determined to be the 20 most religious states in America. The religiousness of a state was determined by the number of citizens who attended religious services, prayed regularly and claimed to believe in God. Not surprisingly, the list was dominated by the Southern states that make up what is known as the "Bible Belt." At the top of the list, Mississippi's high scores made it the clear winner, outdistancing the rest of the country by a significant margin.

The great state of Tennessee lived up to its reputation as the "Buckle of the Bible Belt," coming in at number five in the poll. According to the Pew Forum, 72 percent of Tennesseans believe that religion is very important in their lives—this puts them ahead of South Carolina and just behind Louisiana. When it came to attending worship and praying, Tennesseans ranked sixth, with more than half of the population attending religious services on a weekly basis, and 70 percent of the state's citizens praying every day. When it came to belief in God, Tennesseans took the number four spot.

Not surprisingly, the religious rankings also reflected recent political trends. States that voted Democratic in the 2008 presidential election tended to rank low in the poll, while states that supported Republican candidates tended to rank much higher.

Tighten Your Bible Belt
The "Bible Belt" is a familiar, informal term for a swath of land in the American South that is characterized by socially conservative, evangelical Protestantism. In the past, the term

has been applied to states as far north as the Midwest, but in a study conducted in 1961, researcher Wilbur Zielinkski reduced the geographical reach of the region by narrowing it to include only the states in which Baptist denominations were the predominant religious affiliation. Nowadays, the Bible Belt encompasses most of Texas and Oklahoma, most of the South—including Missouri and southern Indiana and Illinois—and extends all the way to West Virginia, southern Virginia and parts of Maryland. Tennessee's proximity to the center of the span causes residents to claim that they are living in the "Buckle of the Bible Belt."

In Tennessee, the city of Nashville serves as the center for many denominations and their associated businesses and organizations, including the Southern Baptist Convention, the United Methodist Church Publishing House and the National Association of Free Will Baptists. Nashville's reputation as a headquarters for evangelical Christians has earned the city the nickname the "Protestant Vatican." However, the city's growing religious diversity has begun to challenge the grip of fundamental Christianity on the city—Nashville is currently home to six Buddhist communities, five Jewish congregations, five Islamic mosques, one Baha'i center and one Hindu temple and ashram.

Nashville isn't the only religious center in the Volunteer State. Memphis is home to both the Church of God in Christ and the Bellevue Baptist Church, which is one of the largest churches in the Southern Baptist Convention. The international headquarters of the Church of God are located in Cleveland. The city is also the home of Lee University, which is a private university affiliated with the Church of God.

Don't Monkey Around with God!

In 1926, Dayton, Tennessee, played host to the (in)famous "Scopes Monkey Trial." Formally, the case of *Scopes vs. The State of Tennessee* is a landmark American legal case that created a national furor and revealed fault lines between American traditionalists and their more modern counterparts. The trial proved to be one of the most heated and important battles in the ongoing American creation-versus-evolution controversy because the case posed a direct challenge to the Butler Act.

The Butler Act was passed in Tennessee in 1925 after William Bell Riley—the head of the World's Christian Fundamentals Association—brought political pressure to bear on the state legislature, demanding that they pass anti-evolution laws. The act made it illegal to "to teach any theory that denies the story of the Divine Creation of man as taught in the Bible, and to teach instead that man has descended from a lower order of animals."

The American Civil Liberties Union set out to abolish the act, engaging a Tennessee high school teacher named John Scopes. Scopes started intentionally violating the Butler Act by teaching from a textbook that included information about Charles Darwin and the evolutionary ideas he had laid out in his landmark book *On the Origin of Species*. The subsequent courtroom battle was fought by two celebrity attorneys—William Jennings Bryan for the prosecution and Clarence Darrow for the defense—and the trial was broadcast across the country.

Scopes had been actively recruited by a Dayton mining magnate named George Rappleyea, who represented a group of businessmen that felt the trial would result in greater publicity for the small city of Dayton. Scopes took up his role with zeal, purposefully incriminating himself and pushing his students to testify against him for daring to teach them about evolution. The famous American author H.L. Mencken covered the trial with a satirical bent, giving it its simian nickname and reinforcing the sensational nature of the court proceedings. Mencken's writings, along with the popularity of the trial's radio broadcast, made this Tennessee case the predecessor of today's pop-culture courtroom dramas like *Judge Judy*. Scopes was eventually found guilty of violating the Butler Act and ordered to pay a fine of $100. Upon appeal, the ruling was thrown out on a legal technicality. Tennessee repealed the Butler Act in 1967.

Faith in Numbers

Although Tennessee's urban centers are showing large increases in the number of citizens who practice non-Christian faiths, the state is still dominated by faithful Christians who are specifically affiliated with the Baptist denomination. Here's how it all breaks down:

Baptist	39%
Methodist	10%
No religion	9%
Christian	7%
Catholic	6%

Presbyterian	3%
Church of God	2%
Lutheran	2%
Pentecostal/Charismatic	2%
Assemblies of God	1%
Episcopalian/Anglican	1%
Non Denominational Christians	1%
Seventh Day Adventist	1%
Other	3%

TIMELINE OF TENNESSEE'S CIVIL RIGHTS HISTORY

Tennessee has an ambivalent relationship with the Civil Rights Movement. On the one hand, Tennessee—like many states—has a heritage of legal slavery. On the other hand, the practice never developed a stranglehold on the state's economy the way it did in the Deep South, and many communities in Tennessee rejected slavery and openly condemned it. During the struggles of the 1960s, Nashville was a critical flash point of Civil Rights organization, conflict and progress, not to mention that Dr. Martin Luther King Jr. was assassinated in Memphis. Confounding, contradictory, complex and continuing, here's the story:

The Beginning

1865: Ku Klux Klan is formed in Pulaski, Tennessee, after the close of the Civil War.

1884: Early Civil Rights pioneer Ida Wells is forcibly ejected from a train in Memphis for refusing to give up a first-class seat she had purchased in a ladies' train coach. Wells fights back, suing the railroad and drawing national attention to the incident. The action is nearly identical to the protest that Rosa Parks would create 70 years later. Wells goes on to orchestrate a letter-writing campaign to address the problem of lynchings.

1880–1930: During this period, 2805 people are lynched throughout the states of the old Confederacy. Tennessee is not immune from the practice—the state claimed 214 victims of lynching during this period, 177 of them African Americans. In 1892, one of the most infamous incidents occurs in Memphis, when three African American grocers are arrested, dragged from jail and shot to death by a mob.

1930s: The founding of the Highlander Folk School in Grundy County, Tennessee, is a seminal moment in the Civil Rights Movement. Many of the most well-known leaders of the movement—namely Dr. Martin Luther King Jr. and Rosa Parks—learn how to organize, protest and lead at the school. Perhaps even more importantly, the school was a safe haven, where blacks and whites fraternized freely, embodying an ideal that inspired some of the biggest changes in the country's history. Parks' experiences at Highlander inspired her nation-changing bus protest and ensured its success. The school still stands today, now known as Sevier County's Highlander Research and Education Center.

Racial Tensions

1946: The first race riot in American history takes place in Maury County, Tennessee. The riot is sparked by an altercation between a black customer and a white shopkeeper. By that evening, fighting, shooting and rioting breaks out in parts of Columbia, Tennessee. This incident is remembered as being an early case for later–Supreme Court Justice Thurgood Marshall. Marshall defends the accused African Americans in Columbia after they are arrested on charges ranging from rioting to attempted murder. Marshall later admits that the incident left him shaken because he was constantly terrified that he would be lynched for his participation in the trial.

1956: Tennessee's Clinton High School becomes the first Southern high school to integrate. A dozen black students—who would become known as the "Clinton 12"—encounter hostility from their white classmates, and things become heated after pro-segregationists from around the country arrive in droves to protest the Clinton 12 as they enter their new school. Ultimately, Governor Frank Clement calls in state troopers to maintain order.

1959: Even at the dawn of the '60s, African Americans in the predominantly black Fayette and Haywood counties are still not allowed to vote. Most of them are sharecroppers who work on white-owned farms, so when the black workers organize voter-registration drives, they are driven from their shacks and left jobless and homeless. Luckily, a few African American farmers such as Shepard Towles own their own land and set up makeshift tent cities for families in need. In short order, these temporary lodgings on Towles' farm and others house hundreds of homeless black sharecroppers in very hard, unsanitary conditions. Some families spend nearly two years in the tent cities before finding a proper place to live. Although their voting-related efforts are ultimately thwarted, their plight is nationally recognized and plays a part in the passing of the Voting Rights Act of 1965.

The Stormy Sixties

Early 1960s: One of the most important fronts in the battle for Civil Rights is in the cafes and stores of downtown Nashville. In the early years of the 1960s, after months of study, preparation and organization, nearly 100 students stage sit-down strikes in a number of establishments, including Woolworth's, McClellans and Walgreen's. The protests are integrated exercises that include both black and white students, both men and women. Occupying the "white-only" sections of the store's restaurants, the students refuse to leave until they are served. Although they initially receive a chilly reception, the sit-ins eventually change public opinion in Nashville and gain national attention. After a bomb is thrown through the house window of Z. Alexander Looby, the students' lawyer, an integrated group of 3000 strong march to the courthouse and convince Nashville mayor Ben West to promise to integrate Nashville's eating establishments. Within a few weeks, seven stores open their lunch counters to all customers. Dr. Martin Luther King calls the Nashville sit-ins a "model movement."

Dr. Martin Luther King Jr.

Although Tennessee is known as one of the most important centers of the Civil Rights Movement in the South, it is also the site of one of the movement's greatest tragedies. For everyone involved in the Civil Rights Movement, or for those who simply admired Dr. Martin Luther King Jr., the date of April 4, 1968, is one that will not soon be forgotten. While visiting Memphis to show support for a sanitation workers' strike, King finds the city in a state of siege. No garbage had been picked up for over two months, and 4000 National Guard troops hold Memphis in a stranglehold that resembles martial law in certain parts of the city. It was in the midst of this deep, brewing tension that King makes his famous "I Have a Dream" speech at Mason Temple. Coincidentally, the speech contains the phrase: "I may not get there with you, but I want you to know tonight that we as a people will get to the mountaintop." The next day, King is shot and killed while standing on the balcony outside of room 306 at the Lorraine Motel.

On September 28, 1991, the National Civil Rights Museum opens its doors to the public. The Museum is located in the former Lorraine Motel building in Memphis, Tennessee.

WELCOME TO TENNESSEE

HISTORY ON THE MAP

The government of Tennessee has acknowledged 42 major historic sites throughout the state.

Age and Beauty

The Victorian Village is located in Memphis and boasts a number of historic homes dating as far back as 1846. The Benjamin A. Massey home is the oldest home in Memphis. The citizens of Memphis, who recognized the homes' historic value and overwhelming beauty, saved them from the wrecking ball.

The Hunt-Phelann House

In 1830, George H. Whyett built the first part of what would eventually become the 16-room brick house known as the Hunt-Phelann House. Union General Ulysses S. Grant established a strategy room in the parlor of the house while planning the attack on Vicksburg. The Union Army used the house as a hospital, and the Underground Railroad dug a tunnel underneath it. A small, one-room schoolhouse located on the property is thought to be the first school known to have educated blacks in Memphis.

Alex Haley House

Pulitzer Prize-winner Alex Haley, the author of *Roots*, lived in a 10-room bungalow built in 1919, now known as the Alex Haley House heritage site.

Reelfoot Lake

Tennessee's only naturally formed lake is a big draw for its beauty and its history, but Reelfoot wasn't always a part of the state's landscape. The large, 14,000-acre lake—measuring 20 miles in length and seven miles in width—was formed after the New Madrid earthquake of 1811.

The Pinson Mounds

The Pinson Mounds represent one of the state's most significant Native American archaeological sites. There are about 15 mounds located at this National Historic Landmark.

Shiloh National Military Park
During the American Civil War, about 23,746 people were injured or killed in the area that's now called the Shiloh National Military Park. It is believed to have been one of the bloodiest battlefields of the war.

A Trail Through History

The Natchez Trace Parkway, located near Hohenwald, marks an important route used by explorers throughout Tennessee's history. The 442-mile-long parkway was opened for traffic in 1996 and follows the path of early Tennessee settlers, of explorers like Lewis and Clark and of numerous trade and military ventures.

James K. Polk Ancestral Home
The James K. Polk Ancestral Home in Columbia was built in 1816 and is historically valuable if only for its architecture. The fact that it was also the home of the 11th president of the United States just adds to its interest.

DID YOU KNOW?

At that time in U.S. history, James Knox Polk—at the age of 49—was the youngest man ever voted to the presidency. He served one term, from 1845 to 1849, and died three months after Virginia-born Zachary Taylor was voted in as president. The current record for the youngest U.S. president elected to office belongs to John F. Kennedy, who was 43 when he was inaugurated.

Jubilee Hall

The Jubilee Hall of Fisk University is located in Nashville. It was built in 1866 and was initially operated as a "free school for blacks in Nashville." Over the years, it evolved into an institution for higher learning for African Americans.

Nashville's Parthenon
Nashville's Parthenon—an exact, full-sized replica of the Greek Parthenon in Athens—was originally built in 1897 for the Tennessee Centennial Exposition. In 1929, it had to be rebuilt because the original building had some structural problems.

The Belle Meade Plantation

The Belle Meade Plantation is also located in Nashville and was once a thriving, world-renowned thoroughbred stud farm. The home is steeped in history both from the perspective of horses, but also because the building was once the headquarters of Confederate General James R. Chalmers, and the Battle of Nashville was played out on the estate's front lawn.

The Hermitage

The Hermitage, located in the Hermitage area of metropolitan Nashville, was once the home of Andrew Jackson, the seventh president of the United States. It was sold to the state in 1956, 11 years after Jackson's death, and has been preserved as a memorial to the good president ever since.

Tennessee State Capitol
The Tennessee State Capitol in Nashville is considered a "masterpiece of Greek Revival architecture." Construction was completed on the project in 1859 and boasts an early use of structural iron elements paired with an unusual amount of stone construction. The design also incorporates a copy of the choragic monument of Lysicrates.

Cordell Hull Birthplace and Museum

Cordell Hull was born in 1871, earned a law degree, then established the United Nations and posthumously won a Nobel Peace Prize for his efforts, but his beginnings were humble. The Cordell Hull Birthplace and Museum, a rebuilt version of his boyhood home, is located near Byrdstown.

Chickamauga and Chattanooga National Military Park
Chickamauga Creek has the sad history of being the site of one of America's most bloody battlegrounds, where opposing armies fought for control of Chattanooga. Visitors to the Chickamauga and Chattanooga National Military Park can get a refresher course on this period in Tennessee's history.

Rhea County Courthouse

Dayton's Rhea County Courthouse is another brilliant example of early-American architecture, but it's more famous for hosting the Scopes Monkey Trial.

X-10 Graphite Reactor

The X-10 Graphite Reactor at Oak Ridge National Laboratory is the first reactor designed and built to operate continuously.

Andrew Johnson National Historic Site
Located in Greeneville, the Andrew Johnson National Historic Site includes two of the homes where the country's 17th president once lived, as well as the tailor shop where he worked and many of his personal belongings.

The Chester Inn

The first boardinghouse in East Tennessee was the Chester Inn. Built in 1797 in Jonesborough, the inn welcomed a wide assortment of guests throughout the years. It currently houses the National Storytelling Association.

Magnificent Mansion

Blount Mansion, in Knoxville, had tongues wagging when it was being built using only the very best materials available in 1792. Today, it's still a sight to see.

Fort Donelson National Battlefield

Visitors to the Fort Donelson National Battlefield will get an education in Civil War history. The 558-acre site is located off U.S. Highway 79 and was the location of the first solid victory for the North.

Hotel Halbrook Railroad and Local History Museum

The Hotel Halbrook Railroad and Local History Museum is still in the restoration stage, but once completed, the site in Dickson will give visitors a peek into life at the time the hotel was built, back in 1912.

The Sam Houston Schoolhouse

Pioneer, soldier and statesman, Sam Houston helped establish the state of Tennessee, but despite his popularity and the countless living options that were available to him, he preferred to live in a house made of poplar logs he'd hewn himself. The small home was also used as a schoolhouse, where Houston taught students for a fee of eight dollars per term. The Sam Houston Schoolhouse is located in Maryville.

The Carter House

Three generations of the Carter family lived in the Carter House, and the woods and fields surrounding the Franklin home saw a lot of blood spilled during clashes with Union forces during the American Civil War.

The Sparta Rock House
Another pioneer home salvaged and preserved for visitors is the Sparta Rock House. It was built sometime between 1835 and 1839 and is located—where else?—in Sparta.

Marble Springs
In 1941, the state of Tennessee purchased what remained of Governor John Seiver's home— a two-story cabin also known as Marble Springs—and restored it to its original 1796 condition, as it was when Seiver first came to the Knoxville area.

Tipton-Haynes State Historic Site
Colonel John Tipton was the first white resident in what is now called Johnson City. He built his family a log house in 1784, and today, the Tipton-Haynes home is a historic site.

Cragfont
General James Winchester lived in a two-story brick home in what is now called Castalian Springs. He called his mansion Cragfont, and it is now on the list of Tennessee's Historic Sites.

Wynnewood
Wynnewood, another Castalian Springs–area heritage home, is also the "largest extant log structure" in the state and was built in 1828.

Ducktown Basin Museum and Burra Burra Mine
The 17-acre Ducktown Basin Museum and Burra Burra Mine site is located outside of Ducktown. Visitors can tour 10 buildings and learn all about the workings of the copper mine that was in operation from 1899 until 1959.

THE TENNESSEE VALLEY AUTHORITY

Grand Plans

The Tennessee Valley Authority (TVA) was created by a congressional charter in May 1933. The new federally owned corporation was charged with providing navigation, flood control, electricity, fertilizer manufacturing and economic development to the Tennessee valley. Essentially, it was hoped that the TVA would be able to two kill birds with one stone: to provide cheap electricity to rural Tennesseans and to create jobs during the Great Depression while modernizing Tennessee's economy and society. The TVA was the first large regional-planning agency in America—to this day, it's still the biggest. President Franklin Roosevelt imagined that the TVA would have the power of government but with the dynamic flexibility of a private enterprise.

By 1942, construction of 12 hydroelectric projects and a steam plant had employed 28,000 workers. The TVA's generators also powered aluminum plants that were providing the materials for bombs and airplanes during World War II. After the conflict, the TVA completed a 650-mile navigation channel along the length of the Tennessee River. The TVA also became the largest supplier of electricity in the country. Today, the TVA has abandoned possible nuclear power projects for new "green" initiatives.

WELCOME TO TENNESSEE

OAK RIDGE AND THE BIRTH OF THE BOMB

Just a Quiet, Sleepy Town

In the summer of 1942, at the beginning of America's involvement in World War II, a number of government officials wearing army uniforms and insignia of the U.S. Army Corps of Engineers arrived in the small East Tennessee town of Oak Ridge. The men arrived quietly, conducted a preliminary study of area, consulted a number of maps and left just as quietly as they had come. When they returned, however, they brought surveyor's stakes and a grand plan that would win the war and change the world forever. Heeding warnings from many top scientists—including Albert Einstein—that Adolph Hitler was developing a doomsday weapon that employed nuclear fission, President Franklin Roosevelt began to explore the possibility of creating an atomic bomb of his own. After the bombing of Pearl Harbor and America's subsequent entry into the war, the plan was pursued with greater urgency.

In 1942, Brigadier General Leslie R. Groves came to East Tennessee. The newly appointed head of the Manhattan Engineer District, Groves was in charge of locating, planning and building any facilities necessary to beat the Germans to the creation of the atomic bomb. The Oak Ridge area was an ideal site for a number of reasons: the sparsely populated locale made the relocation of the few residents a simple task, and the town itself was located at a safe distance from the proposed nuclear plant. The valleys and ridges in the area also allowed facilities to be separated geographically, in the hopes of minimizing and containing a disaster in any one link in the chain. With plenty of water and the power of the Tennessee Valley Authority (TVA), the site was quickly developed. Between 1942 and 1943, all the necessary evictions in the area had been completed. The finished reservation was approximately 17 miles long and seven miles wide, containing a total area of 59,000 acres.

Growing Pains

The town of Oak Ridge prospered alongside the project, providing the goods and services needed by the scientists, engineers, military personnel and their families. The town itself was designed by a prominent architecture firm—Skidmore, Owings and Merrill—and provided housing for over 8000 people in Oak Ridge. The street names were chosen using an alphabetical system. In one instance, all the roads off Delaware Avenue similarly started with the letter "D," a convenient arrangement in a town full of newcomers. However, the need for accommodations quickly overwhelmed the project, and many of the new residents lived in trailers and barracks while they waited for the town to be finished.

The actual facilities for the scientific side of the Manhattan Project were built by the Stone & Webster Corporation. The final construction included a national headquarters for the project, a graphite reactor and high-tech facilities that allowed for the separation of the fissionable isotopes, which would supply the bomb with its explosive reaction. Construction workers first arrived in Oak Ridge in 1943. One year later, the population of the town had reached an unthinkable 66,000. By 1945, the town was home to 75,000 people, with a staggering 80,000 working on the project at the reservation. Oak Ridge had quickly become the fifth largest city in the state and the sixth largest transit operation in the country, as many workers commuted from Knoxville to build and maintain the facility. Meanwhile, tensions were growing between displaced landowners and the new residents in the town. Area communities also balked at the drain that Oak Ridge put on local resources.

After the War

Work on the project was swift and effective, and the world's first atomic bomb was dropped on Hiroshima, Japan, at 9:00 AM on August 6, 1945. The second bomb fell on Nagasaki on August 9, and Japan surrendered on August 12. While many workers and residents expected a mass exodus, rising tensions of the new Cold War enabled Oak Ridge to maintain a population of about 35,000, and the facilities on the reservation continued to operate. Today, the city of Oak Ridge has taken on a less militaristic atmosphere, and the facility continues to be a thriving research center manned by talented scientists, engineers and a highly trained work force. Oak Ridge has developed a rich cultural life that features a playhouse, a ballet company, a community band and a popular concert series. Currently, research at the facilities, which are now under the direction of the Martin Marietta Corporation, is focused on nuclear power, radioisotopes and the various aspects of nuclear medicine.

TENNESSEE ART MUSEUMS
A Different Kind of Coffeehouse

It was Joel Cheek of Nashville who developed a superior blend of coffee and marketed it through the city's finest hotel—Maxwell House. Cheek sold his company in 1928 for $4 million, and the Cheeks promptly bought 100 acres in West Nashville, where they built a stunning mansion. While America gained a great cup of coffee, Nashville eventually gained a historical home, a fine art museum and breathtaking grounds full of award-winning botanical gardens. The house was completed in 1932 and was an active private residence until 1950, when it was offered up for its new purpose. The property was redeveloped, and the Nashville Museum of Art donated part of its collection to the new project. Cheekwood opened to the public in 1960.

Today, the historical home displays several collections of decorative arts and silver, while numerous galleries—including those from a 2000 addition—display favorites from their collection as well as contemporary installations and video art. The 55-acre garden features new surprises every season, and the Pineapple Room Restaurant is a Nashville institution unto itself.

Tennessee State Museum
In 1937, the Tennessee General Assembly created a state museum for the purpose of collecting mementos from World War I, as well as consolidating other collections from around the state. The first museum was located in the lower level of the War Memorial Building in Nashville. The Tennessee State Museum was eventually moved to its current home in the James K. Polk building in downtown Nashville, where it boasts

over 60,000 square feet dedicated to historic displays and art exhibits. The museum has ongoing exhibits dedicated to subjects like "The First Tennesseans" and "The Civil War and Reconstruction," and it also organizes shows, such as "The Jewish Experience," that travel throughout the state.

The Center of Attention

Housed in a gorgeous Art Deco building in Nashville that was originally a post office created as a Works Progress Administration (WPA) project during the Great Depression, the Frist Center for the Visual Arts is not a museum—they have no collections—but rather, it is an art venue that organizes and displays ongoing cultural programming. The Frist hosts traveling shows from around the world and features exhibits that range from the biggest names in contemporary art to ancient artifacts from lost cultures. In addition to two entire floors of spacious galleries, the center features the ArtQuest Gallery. Staffed by educational professionals, ArtQuest offers a number of interactive activities designed to increase children's understanding of art. The center also hosts guest lectures and film programming, and its cafe has become a popular lunch spot.

Hunting Down a Masterpiece

The Hunter Museum of American Art is located at the top of an 80-foot-high bluff overlooking the Tennessee River. It is one of the highlights of Chattanooga's stunning riverfront, and the view outside the Hunter is almost as good as what you'll see inside its large, meandering galleries. Not only is the Hunter in possession of one of the best collections of American art in the country, but the museum itself—which features an original, historical building with two new, very distinctive additions—is like a tour of over 100 years of American architecture.

WELCOME TO TENNESSEE

A Gift of Art

The Memphis Brooks Museum is the oldest fine art museum in the state of Tennessee. With an extensive collection that ranges from antiquity to the present, the Brooks features a dynamic range of shows, including traveling exhibits from around the world, as well as educational programs. Located in Memphis' historic Overton Park, the sprawling facility includes 29 galleries, two art classrooms, a print study room, a research library and a professional auditorium with state-of-the-art audio-visual equipment.

The Brooks Memorial Art Gallery opened in 1916 with the help of a $100,000 donation from Bessie Vance Brooks. A Beaux-Arts style building, the Georgian marble facility was designed by James Gamble Rogers and was inspired by the Morgan Library in New York City. Following two additions in 1955 and 1973, the institution was renamed the Memphis Brooks Museum of Art in 1983.

WELCOME TO TENNESSEE

A STATE OF LETTERS

James Agee

A journalist, screenwriter, film critic, poet and author, James Rufus Agee was born in Knoxville on November 27, 1909. Agee's father was killed in a car accident when James was only six years old, and Agee was sent away to school, attending various boarding schools, including Saint Andrews in Sewanee. Agee eventually attended Harvard University, where he was the editor-in-chief of the *Harvard Advocate* and delivered his class' commencement ode. Agee later wrote extensively for *Time* and *Fortune* magazines, and he became well known for his film criticism in *The Nation*. Agee married twice, had three children and became a freelance writer in the 1950s. A short-lived foray into screenwriting was cut short by the writer's alcoholism, but he is credited on two classic films—*The African Queen* and *The Night of the Hunter*. Agee died on May 16, 1955. His first novel *Let Us Now Praise Famous Men* is considered a classic of American literature.

DID YOU  KNOW?

In 1957, James Agee was awarded a posthumous Pulitzer Prize for his novel *A Death in the Family*.

Madison Smartt Bell

Born in 1957 and raised near Nashville, Madison Smartt Bell attended both Ensworth School and Montgomery Bell Academy before moving on to the creative writing program at Princeton. After graduating in 1979, Bell worked in New York City as a soundman on a television crew and a security guard in a boutique. He received a masters degree in English and creative writing from Hollins College in 1981.

Highly praised as both a novelist and a short story writer, Bell has received both the Guggenheim and National Endowment for the Arts fellowships. His short fiction has been selected four times for inclusion in the annual *Best American Short Stories* collection, and he has taught at exclusive institutions like Johns Hopkins and the Iowa Writers Workshop. Bell's work has been translated into eight languages.

The Fugitives

The Fugitives were a group of poets and literary critics that formed at Nashville's Vanderbilt University after World War I. Their work was showcased in *The Fugitive*, a literary magazine that they published from 1922 to 1925. *The Fugitive* was a highly influential periodical, and the Fugitives are well known because so many of their members went on to create unforgettable works that have since become classics in the American Literature canon.

- **John Crowe Ransom:** Born on April 30, 1888, Ransom was a poet, essayist, philosopher and social theorist. He was the son of a Methodist minister and grew up in Pulaski. Ransom attended Vanderbilt University and won a Rhodes scholarship that took him to Oxford University in England. After serving as an artillery officer in World War I, Ransom returned to Vanderbilt where he founded the Fugitives and published his two most influential collections of poetry—*Chills and Fever* and *Two Gentlemen in Bonds*.

- **Allen Tate:** Born near Winchester, Kentucky, on November 19, 1899, Tate met the poet Robert Penn Warren while they were both attending Vanderbilt University. Under the tutelage of John Crowe Ransom, Tate joined the Fugitives and became an active contributor to *The Fugitive*. Eventually relocating to live the bohemian life in New York City's Greenwich Village, Tate wrote for *The Nation* and published in *Poetry*. In 1928, he published his most influential poem, "Ode to the Confederate Dead." He was the U.S. poet laureate from 1943 to 1944.

- **Robert Penn Warren:** The best known of the Fugitives, Warren was born on April 24, 1905, in Guthrie, Kentucky. After graduating from Clarksville High School, Warren attended Vanderbilt University, where he joined the ranks of his fellow Fugitives. While Warren's conservative point of view found him defending segregation as an undergrad, he eventually published widely in defense of the Civil Rights Movement during the 1960s. Warren served as the U.S. poet laureate from 1944 to 1945 and won the Pulitzer Prize in 1947 for his famous novel *All the King's Men*. Warren also won Pulitzer Prizes for poetry in 1958 for *Promises: Poems 1954–1956* and again in 1979 for *Now and Then*. Warren is the only writer ever to receive Pulitzers in both fiction and poetry.

 Nashville's current Fugitive Artist Collective takes its name from its literary predecessors.

The Sewanee Review

The oldest literary journal in the United States, *The Sewanee Review* was founded in 1892 and is based out of the University of the South in Sewanee, Tennessee. Publishing poetry, fiction, essays and criticism, *The Sewanee Review* has, over its long tenure, featured many of the most talented voices in writing, including Robert Penn Warren, Flannery O'Connor and Dylan Thomas.

WELCOME TO TENNESSEE

A BRIEF HISTORY OF COUNTRY MUSIC

The Home of Country Music is *Not* Nashville
Although Tennessee has a long, varied and celebrated history with many forms of music, the state is most famously known as the home of country music. Though Nashville—the commercial capital of country—is known as "Music City," the official birthplace of country music is located in the northeast corner of the state along the Virginia border. In 1998, Bristol, Tennessee, was officially recognized by the U.S. Congress as the birthplace of country music because it was the location of what has since become known as the "Big Bang of Country Music." Among country music fans, the "Bristol Sessions" are still spoken of in hushed, reverent tones.

Country music had been commercially available since 1922, but America and the rest of the world had yet to hear the sounds that were being produced in the genre's Appalachian birthplace. Since the only studios that were recording country music at that time were located in New York City, they had no real connection to the genuine music of the countryside. Instead, most "country" music was being cut by popular singers in other genres who would "crossover" to fill the burgeoning demand. In an effort to seek out new talent, record labels like Okeh Records and Columbia Records finally sent their scouts to Tennessee.

Ralph Peer was an experienced producer for the Victor Talking Machine Company. In 1927, he arrived in Bristol with his wife and two sound engineers. They put the word out that they were looking for talented musicians and were overwhelmed with the response they received. Having to schedule night sessions in order to keep up with the number of anxious performers who'd made the trip to Bristol, Peer recorded 76 songs in 19 sessions over the course of two packed weeks.

While the amount of original music cut during the Bristol sessions surely proved bountiful, it was the quality of the talent that made the recordings legendary. The Bristol sessions marked the debuts of both the Carter Family and Jimmy Rodgers, acts who would both go on to establish the foundations of modern country music. Peer's contracts—paying artists a share of royalties on future sales—became a model for the big business of country music in Nashville.

Nashville = Ca$hville
Just as country music began to find its record-buying audience, the Great Depression struck and the entire recording industry suffered a drought in record sales. Luckily for country musicians, a nationwide audience was still available to them via a 50,000-watt radio tower in Nashville. The radio station WSM began broadcasting the Grand Ole Opry in 1925. The legendary variety program featured the best in country music and could be picked up on radios nearly anywhere in

the country. While it was difficult to make a living as a recording artist, one appearance on the stage of the Grand Ole Opry could very easily transform a hopeful artist into a household name.

By the 1950s, country music had grown and evolved, giving birth to western swing, rockabilly and bluegrass. Nashville was not only home to the Grand Ole Opry, but it became a new recording mecca as well. The Nashville sound transformed the little niche of country music into a multimillion-dollar business. Masterminded by producers like Chet Atkins and Owen Bradley, the Nashville sound paired traditional country subject matter with pop-song structure and arrangements that featured multiple vocals, strings and tasteful, musical riffs in place of the extended solos so popular in bluegrass. The result was a broadening of the audience for the music and the beginning of a long-term trend.

DID YOU  KNOW?

In the '90s, Garth Brooks updated the Nashville sound with contemporary pop production and went on to become one of the most popular artists in any genre, *ever*. Nowadays, it's common for rockers like Kid Rock and country songstresses like Taylor Swift to move freely back and forth between the worlds of country and pop music.

SIX LEGENDS OF COUNTRY MUSIC

The Father of Country Music

Known for his trademark yodeling, Jimmy Rodgers was one of country music's first superstar performers. In addition to nicknames like the "Blue Yodeler" and the "Singing Brakeman," Rodgers is often quite simply called the "Father of Country Music." Discovered during the Bristol sessions, Rodgers' recordings of "T for Texas" and "Out on the Mountain" rocketed him to a superstar career that included films, tours and even duets with Louis Armstrong.

Country's First Family

The Carter Family came from southwestern Virginia, but they found fame when they crossed the border to Bristol, Tennessee, in 1927 to record with producer Ralph Peer for the Victor label. In 1928, the Carters recorded a number of their signature tunes, including "Keep on the Sunny Side," "Can the Circle Be Unbroken" and "Wildwood Flower." Their congregational-style singing and Maybelle's revolutionary guitar picking won them legions of fans and allowed the Carters to establish their own radio show.

DID YOU KNOW?

Maybelle's daughter, June, married country legend Johnny Cash in 1968.

The Man in Black

A giant in the genre of country music, Johnny Cash's talent encompassed blues, gospel and rockabilly, and continues to influence artists in every popular genre to this day. Known for his booming baritone and the freight-train rhythms of his signature recordings, Cash's colorless fashion sensibility earned him the moniker the "Man in Black."

Named "J.R." by his parents because they couldn't agree on what to call their new baby boy, Cash was born in Arkansas in 1932. Growing up poor, J.R. started working in cotton fields when he was only five years old. Cash sang and played guitar from an early age. He grew up steeped in the gospel music he learned at church and the popular tunes he heard on the radio. When Cash enlisted in the U.S. Air Force, they wouldn't accept his initials as his first name, so J.R. became John R. Cash.

After his service in the air force, Cash married Vivian Liberto, and the couple moved to Memphis. Cash's original songs won over Sam Phillips at Sun Records—"Hey Porter" and "Cry, Cry, Cry" were early hits for Cash, but his recordings of "I Walk the Line," "Folsom Prison Blues" and "Home of the Blues" cemented Cash's dark, brooding style and found him joining the pantheon of Sun stars that included Carl Perkins, Jerry Lee Lewis and Elvis Presley.

Drugs, alcohol and a relentless touring schedule, however, all took their toll on Cash and led to his divorce from Liberto. Cash eventually recovered from his addictions by becoming a born-again Christian and went on to marry June Carter of the legendary Carter Family. He had his own television variety show in the early 1970s, and his career had a late, massive resurgence in the 1990s with the re-release of his CDs on the American Recordings label. June Carter Cash died in May 2003, and Johnny Cash followed her four months later.

Hank Williams

Hiram King Williams was born in a log cabin in Mount Olive, Alabama, in 1923, but by the time of his premature death in 1953, Hank Williams had firmly established himself as a legendary singer-songwriter whose catalog serves as the foundation for country music to this day. The first performer to earn six encores on the Grand Ole Opry, Williams was also fired by the Opry for his rampant drunkenness. A pioneer of the honky-tonk style, Williams' lively music and charismatic performances disguised a life plagued by illness, pain and addiction.

DID YOU KNOW?

Hanks Williams' last official release before he died was entitled "I'll Never Get Out of This World Alive."

The Coal Miner's Daughter

One of the best-known singer-songwriters in country music, Loretta Lynn's rags-to-riches life story is just as compelling as the 16 number-one hits she racked up during her ongoing career. Just as she sings in the opening lines of her hit "Coal Miner's Daughter," Loretta Webb was born in 1935 to a poor family in Butcher Hollow—a section of the Van Lear mining community in Kentucky. The impoverished lifestyle of the Webbs and their neighbors translated into a lack of modern necessities such as roads, motor vehicles and flushing toilets.

Loretta married Oliver Vanetta "Doolittle" Lynn when she was 13 years old, and they soon moved to a logging community in Custer, Washington. Loretta had four children by the time she was 17, but a year later, she taught herself to play guitar and was discovered while playing in a televised talent contest in Tacoma, Washington. Lynn signed with Zero Records, and her song "I'm a Honky Tonk Girl" was a minor hit, earning Lynn a contract with Decca Records in Nashville. Appearances on the Grand Ole Opry gained Lynn a following, and a string of hits made her a popular star.

However, her songs of the late '60s and '70s espoused an increasingly feminist point of view that was at odds with the rest of country music. Classic hits from this period—including "The Pill," "What Kind of Girl (Do you Think I Am)" and

"Coal Miner's Daughter"—earned Lynn a place among country music's legendary singer-songwriters. While her music career slowed in the '80s, *Coal Miner's Daughter*, the film based on Lynn's autobiography, was a critical and commercial smash that earned Lynn a wider audience beyond country music fans. Loretta Lynn's ranch in Hurricane Mills, Tennessee, continues to be a popular attraction for tourists.

DID YOU KNOW?

Lynn's 2004 comeback album "Van Lear Rose" was produced by Detroit rocker Jack White. It earned Lynn five Grammy nominations and two awards, including Best Country Album.

Hello Dolly

A country music legend and a pop-culture phenomenon, Dolly Parton is a singer-songwriter, multi-instrumentalist, actor, entrepreneur and philanthropist whose talents have earned her a global audience of fans and admirers. Dolly Rebecca Parton was born in the Great Smoky Mountains of Sevier County in 1946. The fourth of 12 children, Parton was raised "dirt poor" in the East Tennessee community of Locust Ridge. Parton's grandfather was a "holy roller" preacher, and the young Dolly grew up singing spiritual songs that she still includes in her set lists today. A child star, Parton sang on local radio as a young girl, recording her first song and appearing at the Grand Ole Opry at the age of 14. Johnny Cash encouraged her to follow her own path, and Dolly started writing hits for other artists and joined the cast of *The Porter Wagoner Show* in 1967.

Wagoner secured a RCA-Victor recording contract for Dolly, and the duo soon had what amounted to a six-year streak of consecutive top-10 singles. Dolly's solo efforts, though, failed to catch on until Wagoner suggested reaching back into the country music canon and covering Jimmie Rodgers' "Mule Skinner Blues." The single led to Parton's first success as a solo performer and saw the subsequent release of such Parton-penned classics as "Coat of Many Colors" and "Jolene." When Parton officially parted ways with Wagoner in 1974, she was so inspired by her respect for her former mentor that she wrote "I Will Always Love You" about their musical friendship. Though many artists have since recorded the song, it became one of the biggest-selling records ever when it was released by Whitney Houston in 1992 for the movie *The Bodyguard* with Kevin Costner.

Parton continued to sell records through the '70s and '80s, proving to be both an influential songwriter and a successful recording artist. In films like *9 to 5*, *The Best Little Whorehouse in Texas* and *Steel Magnolias*, Parton also showed herself to be a legitimate dramatic actress and a particularly talented comedienne. In Tennessee, Parton promotes the Great Smoky Mountains through her family theme park, Dollywood—the number-one tourist attraction in the state. Parton is also a champion of children's literacy and her international Imagination Library delivers a book a month to children all over the U.S., Canada and the United Kingdom. Her 2008 CD *Backwoods Barbie* reached number two on the country charts.

WELCOME TO TENNESSEE

MEN AND WOMEN OF THE MEMPHIS BLUES

Memphis blues music developed as a style in the '20s and '30s. Coming of age in the clubs and bars on Beale Street, the Memphis blues began as an acoustic-guitar-and-jug-band music style that incorporated the swing and syncopation of jazz. Early pioneers like W.C. Handy composed the first popular hits that would bring the blues to a mainstream audience. After World War II, B.B. King transformed Memphis blues into an electric-guitar-based style that still retained a feel for jazz technique, while other artists like Ike Turner pioneered the rhythm-and-blues music that set the stage for rock 'n' roll.

The Father of the Blues

William Christopher Handy was born in Florence, Alabama, in 1873. The son of a preacher, Handy was a deeply religious man all his life. Although Handy credited the church with his early musical education, he was also inspired by the natural sounds he heard near the creeks in the woods near his home—the tunes of chirping songbirds honed his ear for musical composition.

Handy was a highly knowledgeable and educated musician. His parents enrolled him in organ lessons, and he also studied the coronet. He tried not to let his parents find out that he was simultaneously learning "sinful" instruments like the guitar. During young adulthood, Handy found work as a coronetist, trumpeter, singer, bandleader and music teacher. He organized small string orchestras and toured with minstrel shows. During his travels, Handy was introduced to the rural folk music of poor African Americans in the South, and he was haunted by the energy and imagination in their songs.

Handy moved to Memphis with his band in 1909, and he started performing the song "Memphis Blues" in 1912. The song is credited with engendering the foxtrot dance craze, and it also marks the first mainstream popularization of the 12-bar blues form. Handy went on to record other classics like "St. Louis Blues" and became a pioneer as an African American music publisher. W.C. Handy's great contribution to music was his marrying of folk material to his own inventive compositions—he didn't invent the blues, but he transformed them into a force that changed the face of American popular music.

The Uncrowned Queen of the Blues

Born Ida Prather in Toccoa, Georgia, Ida Cox grew up singing in church and became a traveling minstrel performer at a young age. By 1920, Cox was headlining performances in the Southeast, drawing crowds that rivaled those of well-known musicians like "Jelly Roll" Morton. Blues had become a staple for white bands and recording artists, but it wasn't until the 1920s that black artists like Cox were given the opportunity to record the blues. At the height of her creativity, Cox was as famous and influential as legendary singers like Ma Rainey and Bessie Smith. Cox's recording career flourished, and she shared the studio with greats like Fletcher Henderson, Charlie Christian, Coleman Hawkins and Lionel Hampton. While the careers of Rainey and Smith ground to a halt in the 1930s, Cox's entrepreneurship, urban-blues style and over-the-top stage shows kept her career going strong until health issues forced her off the road in the '40s. Cox's vocal skills earned her the nickname the "Uncrowned Queen of the Blues," while her lyrics—which focused on the struggles in the lives of Southern women—made her a songwriting pioneer. Cox died of cancer in Knoxville in 1967.

B.B. King (and Lucille)

In 1925, Riley B. King was born in Itta Bena, Mississippi. The boy's early history is something of a mystery, but it's clear that music was always a big part of his life. Like so many other blues greats, the gospel songs he learned at church would serve as his first musical foundation. However, King was also drawn to playing the guitar, and he bought his first instrument for $15 at the age of 12. After one failed attempt to make a life for himself in Memphis, King returned in 1948 after T-Bone Walker inspired him to get an electric guitar. King worked as a DJ at WDIA in Memphis, where he was known as the "Beale Street Blues Boy"—the name stuck and was eventually shortened to simply "B.B." He toured extensively and cut classics like "Everyday I Have the Blues" with various small labels.

In 1962, King signed with ABC-Paramount Records, a label that promoted artists like Ray Charles and Fats Domino. King flourished, and this golden period yielded his breakthrough

Grammy-winning song "The Thrill is Gone," as well as classic albums like *Live at the Regal* and *B.B. King in London*, which featured a number of Britain's rock royalty, including Ringo Starr, Peter Green and Steve Winwood. King's success also attracted the attention of rockers like Eric Clapton and Keith Richards, and their influence pushed King's elegant style of Memphis blues into the mainstream. King and Lucille—B.B.'s pet name for his guitar—have continued to speak to audiences across genres and around the world for over 50 years, and no one since W.C. Handy has done as much for the Memphis blues as "The King."

B.B. King's Blues Club restaurant and live music venue has five locations—Memphis and Nashville, Tennessee; Orlando and Palm Beach, Florida; and Las Vegas, Nevada.

Ike Turner

Although he is famous—and infamous—for his stormy marriage with Tina Turner, Ike Turner is also one of the most influential guitar players of all time and an early architect of rock 'n' roll.

Ike Turner was born in Clarksdale, Mississippi, on November 5, 1931. His mother was a seamstress and his father was a Baptist minister. At the age of eight, Ike started working at the WROX radio station, keeping an eye on the turntables while the DJs ran out for coffee. By the late 1940s, Turner had formed his own band—the Kings of Rhythm. In 1951, the Kings recorded the song "Rocket 88" at Sun Records in Memphis after Turner's amplifier had just fallen off a parked car—the punctured speaker had to be hastily repaired with paper and tape. The resulting tone was one of the first examples of guitar distortion, and Turner's aggressive style on the recordings earned the song a reputation as being the first rock 'n' roll record. Turner became a talent scout for Sun and other independent labels, and it's through Turner's efforts that other blues acts like Howlin' Wolf,

Sonny Boy Williamson, Elmore James and Otis Rush got signed to recording contracts.

Turner eventually settled into local fame in St. Louis, Missouri, where he met Anna Mae Bullock, a teenage singer from Nutbush, Tennessee. Turner built a musical show around the talented girl, and they began to tour the country as the Ike and Tina Turner Revue. One of the most explosive duos in rock history, Ike and Tina enjoyed 16 years of consistent success from 1960 to 1976, touring constantly and releasing classic recordings such as "River Deep Mountain High," "Nutbush City Limits" and their frenetic cover of a Creedence Clearwater Revival song, "Proud Mary."

Tina left Ike in 1976, and he struggled to maintain a career in the face of crippling chemical dependencies. He later spent four years in jail for drug and weapons charges and was released in 1993. Turner made the most of his freedom, and a long period of sobriety enabled him to take a new run at the charts. In 2007, Turner's album *Risin' With the Blues* earned him his first Grammy as a solo artist. Ike Turner died of a cocaine overdose on December 12, 2007. The chaos of his troubled personal life continues to overshadow his fundamental contributions to American popular music.

DID YOU KNOW?

Ike and Tina Turner were inducted into the Rock and Roll Hall of Fame in 1991.

Memphis Minnie

An influential pioneer as both a singer and a guitarist, Memphis Minnie recorded for four decades and is considered to be one of the great ladies of the Memphis blues.

Lizzie Douglas was born in Algiers, Louisiana, on June 3, 1897. She learned to play both guitar and banjo as a young girl and just as quickly ran away to Memphis at the age of 13. A club and street performer, Douglas even briefly joined the Ringling Brothers Circus. Douglas and her then-husband Kansas Joe McCoy were discovered singing in a Beale Street barbershop by a Columbia Records talent scout, and their first song "Bumble Bee" became a hit in 1929. Adopting the name "Memphis Minnie," Douglas affected a flamboyant lifestyle, arriving at her shows by limousine and wearing heavy bracelets made of silver dollars. By 1939, Douglas had married Little Son Joe Lawlers, and the pair recorded over 100 songs together.

During the 1940s, Douglas created her own vaudeville-style touring company and recorded some of her most enduring songs, including "Nothing in Rambling" and "In My Girlish Days." During this time, she became one of the first blues musicians to champion the electric guitar. She also picked up skills on bass and drum, effectively predicting the electrified sound of the post-war blues in Chicago and Detroit. During her career, Douglas lived in Detroit, Chicago and Indianapolis, but she moved back to Memphis in 1957 as public interest in her music declined.

Memphis Minnie died of a stroke in Memphis in 1973. She is buried at the New Hope Baptist Church Cemetery in Walls, Mississippi, where her grave is marked by a headstone paid for by singer-songwriter and fellow guitarist Bonnie Raitt.

WELCOME TO TENNESSEE

MEMPHIS: CITY OF SOUL

Memphis soul music married a stylish, sophisticated, uptown element to the deeply felt roots of gospel. Intentionally not as slick as the Motown releases being produced in Detroit, Memphis soul always favored impassioned performances and tight, shimmering musicianship over pop music embellishments. During the 1960s and 1970s, Memphis soul became a commercial force while simultaneously providing an inspiring soundtrack for the Civil Rights Movement. Memphis soul changed the way the world listened to music, and it was all thanks to the work of two small independent record labels: Hi Records and Stax.

Hi Records

Originally conceived as a rockabilly label, Hi Records was the brainchild of a group of Sun Studio musicians and a Memphis record storeowner. The label started releasing instrumental music with some success, but it was Willie Mitchell who really put Hi Records on the map, transforming the label into one of the seminal soul music labels. Mitchell brought his prodigious talents as a producer, bandleader, songwriter and talent scout to the table, and his work with a young singer named Ann Peebles broke the label into the national spotlight, producing hits like "Walk Away" in 1969 and "I Can't Stand the Rain" in 1973. However, it was Mitchell's fruitful collaboration with Al Green that made the label, and the singer, immortal. With timeless hits like "Tired of Being Alone," "Take Me to the River" and "Let's Stay Together," Hi became the most important soul label of the 1970s, as well as a legendary contributor to the legacy of Memphis soul.

Stax
In 1960, at the corner of McLemore Avenue and College Street in Memphis, the brother-and-sister team of Jim Stewart and

Estelle Axton converted an old movie theater into a recording studio and record store. The pair had been struggling to get a country label off the ground for three years, and the move into the urban environment of Memphis put the label in the same neighborhood with the talent—not to mention the audience—that would fuel Stax's success as a soul label for years to come. Starting with the Rufus and Carla Thomas hit "'Cause I Love You," the little label was off and running. For the next 18 years, Stax would launch the careers of music legends like Otis Redding, Sam and Dave, Isaac Hayes, Wilson Pickett and Booker T. and the MGs. The studio developed a signature sound owing to the odd acoustics of the old theater building and to the country, blues, gospel and jazz influences that the racially integrated musicians and management brought together. The racial cooperation so evident at the label during such turbulent times was one of its most lasting legacies, and the breakup of the Stax musical family happened when the original Stax label closed its doors in 1975.

Daddy-Daughter Team
Also known as the "World's Oldest Teenager," Rufus Thomas was a singer-songwriter, a DJ and a comedian. During his long career, Thomas discovered B.B. King, taught America to "Do the Funky Chicken" and put Memphis soul music on the map as one of its first bona fide stars. Thomas was the son of a sharecropper and was born on March 27, 1917, in Cayce, Mississippi. His family moved to Memphis, Tennessee, when he was two years old, and Thomas made his show business debut in the role of a frog in a school play at the age of six. Thomas cut records for Sam Phillips at Sun Studios in the '50s, but it was a duet with his daughter, Carla, that would make them both stars.

Carla Thomas was born on December 21, 1942. Raised in a musical household, Carla was a member of the Teen Town Singers amateur radio group by the time she was attending high school. When she was just 18, Carla and Rufus released "Cause I Love You" on the Stax record label. The success of the song launched both of their careers and secured Stax a distribution deal with Atlantic Records. Carla Thomas followed up with her biggest hit, "Gee Whiz (Look at His Eyes)"—the song broke into the Top 10 and landed her a spot on *American Bandstand*. While she never repeated this success, it still earned her the nickname "Queen of Memphis Soul."

Carla Thomas continued to record notable releases into the '70s and still performs to this day. Rufus Thomas also released new records sporadically and scored hits with songs like "Walking the Dog" in 1963 and "The Breakdown" in 1971. Rufus Thomas died of heart failure in 2001.

The Reverend
The sixth of 10 children, Albert Greene, like Rufus Thomas, was the son of a sharecropper. He was born in Forrest City,

Arkansas, on April 3, 1946. Even as a young man, Greene was a talented singer and a hard worker. Performing with various bands and combos as a child and a teenager, Al Greene and the Soul Mates released the single "Back Up Train" on their own Hot Line Music Journal label in 1967, scoring a hit on the R&B charts. Greene then cut a solo record that faired rather poorly, but in 1969, Willie Mitchell signed Greene to Hi Records. After Green dropped the "e" from his last name, he blasted off to meteoric success, encountering personal tragedy as well as spiritual transformation.

Mitchell encouraged Green to sing with his own voice instead of trying to emulate James Brown and Sam Cooke. Green took the advice to heart, and by the 1970 release of his second album, *Al Green Gets Next to You*, Green had found massive success. Subsequent releases like *Let's Stay Together* and *Al Green Explores Your Mind* added to Green's legend, yielding classic songs like "Take Me to the River" and "Tired of Being Alone."

Along with fame came fortune, women and cocaine. Green lived fast and loose until 1974, when he was attacked by a girlfriend who dumped boiling grits on him while he was in the shower and then took her own life with his gun. The incident left Green with third-degree burns and a new lease on life. He gave up the women and the drugs and became a minister. Although he continued to tour, a nearly tragic stage fall in 1979 prompted Green to hang up popular music to focus on singing gospel music and preaching in his church. Thankfully, the Reverend had a change of heart and returned to popular music in 1988. His album *Lay it Down* won two Grammy awards in 2008. Praise the Lord!

DID YOU KNOW?

Reverend Al Green's church is known as the Full Gospel Tabernacle Church.

The Big "O"

The "King of Soul" was born on September 9, 1941, in Dawson, Georgia. While he was still a young boy, Otis Ray Redding Jr. and his family moved to Macon, Georgia, where the youngster grew up singing in the church choir. Redding eventually became the lead singer in the band of the guitar-playing showman Johnny Jenkins.

In 1962, the regional popularity of Jenkins' records earned him a session at Stax Records in Memphis, and Redding auspiciously tagged along as his driver and roadie. During the session, Redding insisted to anyone who would listen that he should be allowed to sing a song. By the time Jenkins had finished his session, Redding had so thoroughly annoyed the Stax staff that they gave him the microphone just to shut him up. Redding made the most of the opportunity, blowing everyone in the room out of their seats with a heartfelt song he'd written himself. "These Arms of Mine" would go on to be his first solo hit, and Redding would go on to be Stax's biggest star because of songs like "(Sittin' On) The Dock of the Bay." Redding is forever remembered as being the "heart and soul of Stax."

Booker T. and the MGs

You can't talk about the Memphis sound without talking about Booker T. and the MGs. In fact, in the case of Stax Records, there wouldn't have been much "sound" at all if not for this stellar band. The MGs are named after the stylish sports car and after Booker T. Jones, the band's charismatic organist. In addition to Jones, the MGs' lineup in 1962 included Steve Cropper on guitar, Lewie Steinberg on bass and Al Jackson Jr. on drums. One day that summer, a spontaneous jam session in the studio was recorded. The result was so thrilling that Stax released it as a single—"Green Onions" became the MGs' first hit and was an instant soul classic.

While the band continues to record and tour to this day, their greatest legacy was playing as the de-facto house band for all the artists who recorded at Stax. The sign outside the Stax studio read "Soulsville USA," and it was largely because of Jones, Cropper, Steinberg, Jackson and Donald "Duck" Dunn—who later replaced Steinberg—that the little label became an international musical treasure. Among the singles that the MGs performed, wrote, arranged or produced are such classics as "Hold On, I'm Coming," "Soul Man," "(Sittin' On) The Dock of the Bay," "Walkin' the Dog" and many more.

DID YOU  KNOW?

Steve Cropper and Donald "Duck" Dunn are in John Belushi and Dan Akroyd's backup band in the film *The Blues Brothers*.

WELCOME TO TENNESSEE

SUN RECORDS: THE CRADLE OF ROCK 'N' ROLL

The House that Sam Built

Originally a pioneering label that had already had some success selling black R&B music to a white audience, Sun Records began signing white rock 'n' roll acts after the label popularized the new music through its association with Elvis Presley. Sam Phillips opened his Memphis Recording Service in 1950. The following year, he cut "Rocket 88" with Ike Turner and the Kings of Rhythm, but it was credited to the fictional group Jackie Brenston and his Delta Cats. The single is now considered to be the first rock 'n' roll song, and it pointed the way toward Sun Records' future.

The Sun Records label was founded in 1952 and, along with Turner, black blues artists like Howlin' Wolf and Rufus Thomas gave the label its early start. On July 5, 1954, an aspiring electrician stopped by the studio to make a record for his mother's birthday. The resulting single "That's All Right," backed with "Blue Moon of Kentucky," began the career of Elvis Presley and turned the little label into a legend. Shortly after Presley's success, Sun signed a number of new, white rock 'n' roll artists, and soon the Sun label—with its distinctive logo—was synonymous with its biggest stars: Elvis Presley, Roy Orbison, Johnny Cash, Jerry Lee Lewis and Carl Perkins. By 1955, Phillips had sold Presley's contract to RCA Victor Records for $35,000 because of financial trouble, and the label was eventually sold in 1969. Sun Entertainment Corporation is now based in Nashville, where they continue to license the re-releases of these classic recordings.

The Killer

On September 29, 1935, a poor family in Ferriday, Louisiana, was blessed with a young boy who would go on to be one of the best-known—and controversial—musicians of the 20th century. Lewis was originally turned down by the Grand Ole Opry in Nashville, leading him to audition for Sun Records in Memphis in 1956, where he began recording his own material and playing as a session man. By 1957, Lewis had cemented his legend with hits like "Whole Lotta Shakin' Goin' On" and "Great Balls of Fire." He was an electrifying performer who was known for kicking his piano bench across the stage and standing on his instrument while leering at his audience. In 2009, Jerry Lee Lewis was the opening performer at the

Rock and Roll Hall of Fame's 25th Anniversary Concert at Madison Square Garden in New York.

DID YOU KNOW?

Jerry Lee Lewis, evangelist Jimmy Swaggart and country crooner Conway Twitty are all cousins.

The Man Behind the Shades

Roy Kelton Orbison was born in Vernon, Texas, on April 23, 1936. Orbison was born nearly blind and wore thick, powerful glasses all his life. His father gave him a guitar at the age of six, and young Roy became obsessed with country artists like Lefty Frizzell and Hank Williams. Orbison was soon appearing on local radio shows and at live events. In 1955, his Teen Kings band did a radio show with Johnny Cash, who suggested that Orbison should audition for Sun Records. Although the Teen Kings scored a contract, they quickly broke up, and Orbison struggled at Sun Records before quitting music completely in 1958.

It was at Monument Records in Nashville that Orbison became a legend. After many experiments, Orbison created a sound that paired his ethereal, operatic vocals with sophisticated arrangements and themes of romantic despair. Classic hits like "Only the Lonely," "Crying" and "Running Scared" are now a part of the rock 'n' roll canon, and the man behind those legendary shades is a pop-culture icon. The late '80s found Orbison topping the charts with his new band, the Traveling Wilburys, featuring Tom Petty, Jeff Lynne, Bob Dylan and George Harrison. The success of the project led to Orbison's last solo record, *Mystery Girl*. The single "You Got It" reached number nine on the Billboard Hot 100. Orbison died of a heart attack in Hendersonville, Tennessee, on December 6, 1988.

The King

Elvis Aron Presley was born in a two-room house in Tupelo, Mississippi, on January 8, 1935. His identical twin, Jesse Garon, was stillborn. When he was 10 years old, Elvis took fifth place in a talent contest at the Mississippi-Alabama Fair and Dairy Show. He won five dollars and his parents bought him a guitar a few months later. The family moved to Memphis in 1945. Presley and his guitar were inseparable, and by the time he was in high school, he had started to grow his trademark sideburns and wear flashy clothes. In 1954, while employed as a truck driver for Crown Electric, Presley recorded "That's All Right" at Sun Studio. This first recording started the rock 'n' roll revolution that made Elvis the biggest star in the world.

By November 1955, Elvis had signed a new contract with RCA-Victor, and "Heartbreak Hotel" became a number-one hit in 1956. In 1957, Elvis was drafted into the army and his career necessarily stalled. Elvis had made his cinematic debut in the western musical *Love Me Tender* in 1956. His movies were panned critically but always made healthy profits—however, the schlocky productions were blamed for Elvis' fading popularity, and popular music in the 1960s left him behind.

In 1968, a guest appearance on NBC featured live segments that showed Elvis decked out in black leather, singing and playing guitar with the same raw power that had won him his earliest fans. The comeback inspired him to record hits like "In the Ghetto" and "Kentucky Rain." In 1969, Presley signed a multimillion-dollar, five-year contract with the International Hotel in Las Vegas. Despite his continuing success, Presley developed debilitating chemical dependencies and severe weight problems, and he died on August 16, 1977.

Elvis' later performances found him executing karate moves on stage. Presley studied the martial art and was first introduced to it while serving in the army.

WELCOME TO TENNESSEE

TENNESSEE'S TOP TELEVISION AND SCREEN STARS

The Silver Screen

Tennessee is a place that many stars of the big and small screens claim as home. In Tennessee today, you are just as likely to meet a movie star as you are a country singer. Here is a constellation of Tennessee's biggest stars:

☛ **Cybill Shepherd:** Born in 1950, the sexy star grew up in Memphis before her breakthrough, big-screen role in the racy *The Last Picture Show*. Shepherd became a household name after portraying the character of Maddie Hayes on the television hit *Moonlighting*.

WELCOME TO TENNESSEE

- **Dinah Shore:** Born Frances Rose Shore, Dinah celebrated her original birthday in Winchester, Tennessee, on February 29, 1916. An accomplished singer, actress and talk show host, Shore won nine Emmys, a Peabody Award and a Golden Globe.

- **George Hamilton:** The always-tan, playboy actor was born in Memphis on August 12, 1939.

- **Jack Hanna:** Wildlife entertainment pioneer "Jungle" Jack Hanna is known for his many television appearances on shows like *Late Night with David Letterman*. Hanna is the creator of *Jack Hanna's Animal Adventures*.

- **Jerry Lawler:** Known as "The King" of professional wrestling, Lawler's early career blossomed in the active pro-wrestling scene in his hometown of Memphis. In the 1980s, Lawler became a cult celebrity for his hoax wrestling matches with oddball comic Andy Kaufman.

- **Johnny Knoxville:** Born March 11, 1971, Phillip John Clapp took the name of his hometown and crashed into America's living room with the hit MTV series *Jackass*. The show spawned three films, and Knoxville has also starred in the movie version of the television series *The Dukes of Hazzard*.

- **Kathy Bates:** Before bringing the world *Misery* in 1990, the popular actress was born in Memphis on June 28, 1948.

- **Megan Fox:** The sexy siren from the *Transformers* movies was born in Oak Ridge, Tennessee, and grew up in Rockwood. Men everywhere will agree that she is the second most atomic thing to ever come out of Oak Ridge.

- **Miley Cyrus:** Did you know Hannah Montana calls Nashville home? Miley Cyrus was born in Music City in 1992, and this singing starlet followed in her father's—country singer Billy Ray Cyrus—footsteps, becoming a huge star in her own right.

WELCOME TO TENNESSEE

- **Minnie Pearl:** Born in Centerville on October 15, 1912, Sarah Ophelia Colley Cannon was a singer and comedienne best known for her appearances on television's *Hee Haw*.

- **Morgan Freeman:** Academy Award-winning actor and ubiquitous narrator, Morgan Freeman was born on June 1, 1937, in Memphis.

- **Oprah Winfrey:** Although she was born in Mississippi, Oprah moved to Nashville when she was 14. She eventually graduated from Tennessee State University and won the title of Miss Black Tennessee while she was a college freshman.

Winfrey spent part of her early career as a local television news anchor in Nashville.

- **Reese Witherspoon:** Born in New Orleans, Witherspoon moved to Nashville at the age of five. Witherspoon still has a house in Tennessee—perhaps that's where she keeps the Oscar she won in 2006 for her portrayal of June Carter in the Johnny Cash biopic *Walk the Line*.

- **Samuel L. Jackson:** This popular actor is best known for his work with fellow Tennessean, Quentin Tarantino. Jackson moved to Chattanooga when he was a young child.

- **Shannen Doherty:** This TV bad girl called Memphis home before she changed her zip code to 90210.

- **Quentin Tarantino:** This cinematic wünderkind was born in Knoxville in 1963. This Oscar winner is famous for his shockingly violent, yet bitingly funny films.

Tarantino Picks on Tennessee

Movie master Quentin Tarantino was born in Knoxville, and though many people don't associate the talented director with the Volunteer State, he seldom makes a movie without including a reference to Tennessee:

- Tarantino's soundtracks often feature country music. The film *Jackie Brown* featured Johnny Cash singing "Tennessee Stud."

- In *Pulp Fiction*, Butch was meeting his connection in Knoxville, where his great-grandfather bought the gold watch.

- The spit-can that Budd uses in *Kill Bill 2* is labeled Oak Ridge Coffee. Oak Ridge is a town in Tennessee about 15 miles from Knoxville.

- In *Kill Bill 2*, Samuel L. Jackson plays the piano player at the wedding rehearsal. He mentions having played with Memphis legends like the Bar-Kays and Rufus Thomas.

- Rosario Dawson convinced Quentin Tarantino to let her cut her hair like pinup icon Betty Page for her part in *Death Proof*. Betty Page was from Nashville. Uma Thurman sports a similar 'do in the Tarantino classic, *Pulp Fiction*.

- Tarantino wrote the script for the film *True Romance*. In the film, Christian Slater's character Clarence regularly turns to the ghost of Elvis Presley for guidance.

- Tarantino was the executive producer of *Daltry Calhoun*. The film starred fellow hometowner Johnny Knoxville, and it took place in the city that is the comedian's namesake.

- Lebanon, Tennessee, is the setting for the second half of Tarantino's film *Death Proof*. The newspaper held and referenced by the character, Zoe, gives it away.

- In *Inglorious Basterds*, Brad Pitt plays Aldo Raine, a hillbilly-moonshiner from Maynardville, Tennessee, who leads a group of Jewish-American soldiers on a Nazi killing spree during World War II.

WELCOME TO TENNESSEE

TENNESSEE AND THE VISUAL ARTS

Portrait Anyone?

While Tennessee is most known for its tremendous contributions to music and recording, the state has also developed a vibrant art scene and has even produced a star or two. As a largely rural state with a lack of concentrated wealth and education, Tennessee didn't begin as a haven for artists or collectors, and it was only when a market for portrait painting began to spring up that Tennessee's history with the visual arts really began in earnest.

WELCOME TO TENNESSEE

- Ralph E.W. Earl was likely Tennessee's first full-time artist. After acquiring a patron in Nashville in 1817, Earl painted a portrait of Andrew Jackson and even proceeded to marry into the soon-to-be president's family, living with Jackson at the Hermitage for a time. Earl continued his portrait work in Nashville until 1829, when he followed Jackson to Washington, DC, where he lived at the White House.

- Washington Bogart Cooper opened his Nashville studio in 1830, where he kept a very busy schedule. Cooper eventually earned the nickname the "Man of a Thousand Portraits." Cooper's brother, William, also became a portrait artist, working out of Memphis.

- John Wood Dodge had a reputation as Tennessee's premier portrait miniaturist. An in-demand artist, Dodge's commissions found him traveling all over when he wasn't at home working in his Nashville studio.

- William Harrison Scarborough was the leading artist in East Tennessee from 1845 until after the Civil War.

- George Dury was a German portrait painter who moved to Nashville in 1850. Dury made a big splash with a portfolio full of work he had done at the behest of various European royals.

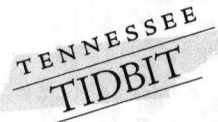 The War of 1812 gave rise to artistic, panoramic landscape painting in Tennessee.

Luscious Landscapes
As Tennessee's economy grew, so did its art market. Eventually, painters who included landscapes and the grounds of estates in their portraits were in great demand, and soon, talented landscape artists began to find growing interest in their work.

- The overmantel caprices at the Carter Mansion in Elizabethton were completed in 1790, and they likely represent the earliest known examples of landscape painting in Tennessee.

- James Cameron was a painter of Scottish descent who settled in Chattanooga after securing a wealthy patron. Best known for work that combined large groups in expanding vistas, many of Cameron's pieces depicted newly completed buildings as well as expressing a kind of state pride in the triumph of progress and civilization over Tennessee's still-wild areas.

- Some of Tennessee's earliest landscapes were scientific, topographical renderings—not works of art. Charles Alexandre Lesueur drew elaborate sketches of both the Mississippi and Cumberland Rivers in 1828 and 1832. The original sketches reside in Le Havre, France. They have never been displayed in the state of Tennessee.

- John H.B. Latrobe is credited with completing the first painting of Memphis in 1832.

- In 1858, a benefit exhibit of 350 paintings was held at the state capitol. Sales of the work were successful enough to allow the purchase of Washington Cooper's portrait series of Tennessee governors by the Tennessee Historical Society.

- Before the Civil War, art instruction was only given to schoolgirls as a kind of fashionable activity.

DID YOU  KNOW?

Most landscape artists preferred to use watercolors as they were the most convenient medium for these often-traveling artists.

Later Artistic Notables

☛ After the Civil War, Tennessee's art market grew back bigger than ever, with new fashions and in-demand art expanding to include still-lifes, "Negro studies," allegories like those of Carl Gutherz, and landscape and genre painting in the realistic, Barbizon style that had originally developed in the French village of the same name.

☛ Art was one of the first careers that a woman was allowed to pursue in Tennessee. In 1887, Alda Lutz commenced a commercial art career after receiving training in Europe and continued to paint until her death in 1931.

- Gilbert Gaul won a bronze medal at the Paris Exposition of 1889 for his historical genre painting *Charging the Battery*. Gaul is known as the first important Tennessee artist who was not a portrait painter.

- Tennessee artist Willie Betty Newman won honorable mention at the Paris Exposition of 1900.

- Catherine Wiley was the state's best-known Impressionist painter. Her most famous works portray female subjects in quiet interior spaces. Her best-known painting is *Woman in Blue at a Desk*. Her painting *The Willow Pond* now resides at the Metropolitan Museum of Art in New York.

Into the 20th Century

- Impressionism didn't catch on in Tennessee until it was passé in Europe, and the style's popularity continued to linger well into the 1930s. Tennessee resisted post-Impressionist works as well and would barely accept even semi-abstract work until the 1960s.

- Carroll Cloar was a regionalist painter whose work gained popularity during the resurgence in landscape painting during the 1930s. During the Great Depression, many Tennessee artists were given federal commissions to paint murals in 30 Tennessee post offices.

- African American art and artists in Tennessee made their first, recognized contributions in the middle of the 20th century. Aaron Douglas was the first important African American artist in Tennessee, and he was also the first artist to focus his subject matter on black culture. Douglas made his reputation as a painter of the Harlem Renaissance whose geometric, stylized work recalled African folk art. Douglas was on the faculty of Nashville's Fisk University from 1936 until 1969. Douglas painted important architectural murals on the school's campus, and the Fisk galleries are recognized as the first in the country to focus primarily on work by African Americans.

- Brothers Beauford and Joseph Delaney were African American modern painters who were born and raised in Knoxville.

- Red Grooms is Tennessee's best-known contemporary artist still living today.

- Robert Ryman is a major painter who is associated with the minimalist and monochrome painting movements. Ryman was born in 1930 in Nashville, where he was raised and eventually graduated from the Peabody College for Teachers in 1950. A conceptual artist who is concerned with materials more than subject matter, Ryman is known for the textured surfaces of his all-white paintings.

- William Eggleston was born in Memphis in 1939. He attended the Webb School in Bell Buckle, Tennessee, and eschewed sports and outdoor activities for artistic pursuits. Eggleston attended Vanderbilt University, Delta State College and the University of Mississippi over the course of five years but never earned a degree. A friend at Vanderbilt gave this artist his first camera. Eggleston's 1974 exhibition at the Museum of Modern Art in New York is recognized as a milestone display, leading to the acceptance of color photography as a legitimate fine art medium.

William Eggleston played the role of Jerry Lee Lewis' father in the music biopic *Great Balls of Fire.*

WELCOME TO TENNESSEE

TENNESSEE'S LEGENDARY LADIES

Tennessee has had many heroes in social and political movements and in the arts. However, a handful of Tennessee women represent more than the best of their field. These ladies broke all the barriers and defined what was possible for women at a time when most industries and movements were run strictly by men. Sexy, smart, tough and tender, these women have left their mark on civil rights, the arts, politics and the way that we define women and the roles they play to this day.

Tina Turner

In a state chock full of electrifying performers, Turner is probably only second to Elvis Presley in the overall effect she had on pop culture. A singer and dancer known for her ferocious stage performances, Turner has won numerous music recognitions, including seven Grammy Awards. She has also sold 50 million records and has made several movies and music videos.

Born Anna Mae Bullock on November 26, 1939, in Nutbush, Tennessee, Turner grew up surrounded by the music that thrived in the black churches, cafes and juke joints that peppered West Tennessee. By the age of nine, Anna Mae had become a singer in her own right, finding her voice as a rhythm-and-blues icon. By the late 1950s, Anna Mae had moved to St. Louis, Missouri, where she auditioned as a singer for Ike Turner's band. By 1960, they were a couple and started billing themselves as the Ike and Tina Turner Revue. One of the most popular acts of the 1960s, the Revue scored worldwide hits and influenced legendary rock bands like the Rolling Stones.

By 1976, Ike and Tina split amid charges of domestic assault. Tina then went solo, and her 1984 album *Private Dancer* became one of the biggest records of the decade, selling more than 10 million copies and winning her three Grammy Awards. The biopic *What's Love Got to do With It?* was based on her autobiography *I, Tina*. Together, the film and the book cemented Turner's reputation as a world-class entertainer and an icon of female strength and character.

Marilou Awiakta

A poet, storyteller and essayist of Cherokee descent, Awiakta was born in Knoxville and raised in Oak Ridge. Her creation of a unique fusion of her native roots, Appalachian culture and science has brought Awiakta recognition from around the world. Her books *Abiding Appalachia: Where Mountain and Atom Meet* and *Rising Fawn and the Fire Mystery* were chosen for the global tour of the U.S. Information Agency's exhibit "Women in the Contemporary World." Awiakta received the Distinguished Tennessee Writer Award in 1989 and the Outstanding Contribution to Appalachian Literature Award in 1991. Her third book, *Selu: Seeking the Corn-Mother's Wisdom*, was published in 1993 and addresses contemporary issues through the lens of Cherokee philosophy. A quote from the book was engraved on the River Wall of the Bicentennial Capitol Mall State Park in Nashville. The *Selu* audiobook was nominated for a Grammy Award. Awiakta's writings continue to remind modern citizens of the deep culture and wisdom of the native Tennesseans.

Callie House

Born Callie Guy into a slaveholding in Rutherford County in 1861, Callie House—her name by marriage—became known as one of the most outspoken political activists in Tennessee, fighting for reparations during the Jim Crow era that plagued the South with legalized segregationist policies after the Civil War.

As a mother of five children, House took in laundry to make ends meet and eventually moved her family to Nashville, looking for better economic circumstances. Along with a handful of other activists, House founded the National Ex-Slave Mutual Relief, Bounty and Pension Association in 1894. The organization sought much-needed capital for freed slaves and attempted to provide resources on a local level while simultaneously agitating for relief and redress on a national level. The group was unique in this multi-tiered approach and for its inclusion of members and supporters regardless of their religion, race or financial standing. Initially, the group faced resistance on many fronts and quickly found themselves under surveillance by the U.S. Pensions Bureau. Undeterred, House then tried, unsuccessfully, to sue the U.S. Treasury Department for $68,073,388.99 in cotton taxes traced to Texas slave labor.

In 1916, Postmaster General A.S. Burleson sought an indictment against House, leading to charges of mail fraud. While it was clear that House—still living in her original, modest Nashville home—hadn't profited from her efforts, and although the group's literature was very clear when it came to the issue of donations, an all-white, all-male jury sentenced House to a year and a day in a Jefferson, Missouri, penitentiary. House's efforts—and the dubious tactics of her opponents—foreshadowed the Civil Rights Movement of the 1960s, and her grassroots organizing within a paternalistic, white-supremacist culture made her a great pioneer in African American culture.

Callie House died on June 6, 1928. Her unmarked grave is in Nashville's Mount Ararat Cemetery.

Betty Page

Betty Mae Page was born in Nashville on April 22, 1923. The product of a broken home that included sexual abuse, Page cared for her younger siblings from a young age, even residing in an orphanage with them for a year at one point. As a teen, Page learned to sew and do her own makeup as she and her sisters imitated the movie stars they admired. Page took a bachelor of arts degree from George Peabody College in 1944, but her sights were already set on stardom. After a short marriage to her high-school sweetheart, Page moved to New York, where she soon found success as a semi-nude model in special magazine clubs that skirted obscenity laws. She became a huge success in this fetishistic underworld while also studying acting, performing off-Broadway and on television, and starring in silly, mildly risqué films like *Teasarama*.

By the mid 1950s, Page was the top pin-up model in New York City, and it wasn't long before *Playboy* magazine came a-calling. Betty Page was the Playmate of the Month in

January 1955. By this time, she was known as the "Queen of the Pin-Up Girls" and found herself in demand for several years, frequently posing nude but never involved in explicit, sexual content. On the contrary, it was Page's fun, flirty, energetic sensibilities that made her an icon of sexuality at a time when America was just beginning to embrace a more robust attitude toward sex. Her trademark bangs and outrageous self-made costumes made her into a male fantasy as well as a female role model. As evidenced by a strong resurgence in the 1980s, Page's image has had an immeasurable impact on sexuality, fashion, music and film all over the world. Betty Page died on December 11, 2008.

TENNESSEE'S ARCHITECTURAL ICONS

Greek to Me

The centerpiece of Nashville's Centennial Park, the Parthenon is a full-scale replica of the historic Parthenon in Athens, Greece. The building was commissioned for Tennessee's 1897 Centennial Exposition, and it contains a 42-foot statue of the goddess Athena, which is also a replica of a Grecian original. The statue, which is completely covered in gold leaf, was added in 1990 and is the largest indoor sculpture in the western world. The Parthenon also serves as an art museum, with a permanent collection that includes 63 paintings by American artists from the 19th and 20th centuries. The Parthenon holds regular exhibits in its gallery spaces, featuring contemporary artists from around the world.

WELCOME TO TENNESSEE

DID YOU  KNOW?

Nashville was the first city in the South to institute a public school system. Because of the numerous colleges and universities in the city, Nashville has earned the nicknamed the "Athens of the South."

Belle Meade Mansion

The mansion is part of the historic Belle Meade Plantation, which is located just west of Nashville. Built in 1853 by General William Giles Harding, the plantation was famous worldwide for its breeding of championship thoroughbred horses, and the grounds grew to encompass 5400 acres. The Civil War brought hard times to Belle Meade and part of the Battle of Nashville was fought in the mansion's front yard—bullet holes in the stone columns are still visible today. By the turn of the century, the property had been auctioned off, and the last of the family had moved away from the plantation. The grounds became the present-day city of Belle Meade, while the mansion, eight out-buildings and 30 acres were made public property in 1953.

Walk Like an Egyptian

Although the building has burned down twice—in 1832 and again in 1848—the present incarnation of the Downtown Presbyterian Church in Nashville was designed by William Strickland in 1851. One of the best surviving examples of Egyptian revival architecture—a style inspired by Napoleon's survey of Egypt in the late 1700s—in the world, the space features a huge perspective painting of a hall of columns, walls painted with desert flora and Egyptian motifs, as well as many iterations of the winged-disc symbol of the Egyptian god Amun-Ra. To boot, the space behind the altar is dominated by a massive organ that boasts 2709 pipes!

Wright Again

This landmark in Chattanooga is the only Frank Lloyd Wright–designed home in the entire state. Located on Missionary Ridge, the house was commissioned by Seamour and Gerte Shavin in 1949. Wright designed the home with the overarching theme that it should appreciate and respect nature. A so-called "Usonian" house, Wright did away with unnecessary structural elements, creating an open floor plan based on a grid. He also made use of native materials and included large windows to take advantage of natural heating and cooling options. The focal point of the home is a large stone fireplace in the living room, and the exterior is decked out in red cypress and crab orchard stone.

The Seamour-Shavin House is one of the few Wright-designed homes still occupied by its original owners.

Ducks Passing

Famous for the ducks that live on its roof, the Peabody is a luxury hotel in downtown Memphis. Now in its second iteration, the Peabody was originally built in 1925. Designed by Walter W. Ahlschlager, the hotel boasts an Italian Renaissance style, and an old saying claims that "The Mississippi Delta begins in the lobby of the Peabody Hotel." After the hotel was closed in the early 1970s, it reopened in 1981 after undergoing several renovations—the restoration kicked off a downtown revitalization that continues in Memphis today.

Every day, a "Duck Master" leads the ducks from their rooftop perch down to the lobby in an elevator. They are accompanied by John Phillip Sousa's "King Cotton March" as they waddle across a red carpet to swim in the hotel's fountain. They are returned to the penthouse precisely at 5:00 PM.

WELCOME TO TENNESSEE

DID YOU  KNOW?

Nashville's Hermitage Hotel features a men's room in its Oak Room bar that regularly wins national polls as the best restroom in America. The facility has an Art Deco theme, featuring leaded-glass tiles, terrazzo floors and a shoeshine station. It also boasts a door that formerly led to a secret tunnel connected to the State Capitol building. Politics, booze and ladies, oh my!

Blount Mansion, Knoxville

Built in the 1792, the Blount Mansion is a patchwork of America at that time: a Knoxville home built with North Carolina lumber and glass from Richmond, Virginia. This magpie-like style of construction reflects William Blount's role as a North Carolina statesman, a man who served in Congress under the Articles of Confederation and was familiar with all of America's territories during that period. Knoxville didn't exist when the home was built, and the mansion made the area the de facto capitol of the Southwest Territory. The Tennessee State

Constitution was drafted at the house, and the role this location played in the birth of the state has made it "the most important historical spot in Tennessee." Blount was a delegate to the Constitutional Convention, and his role as a signatory of the U.S. Constitution saved the home from being turned into a parking lot in 1925. The property is now recognized as a National Historic Landmark.

The Mother Church

Also known as the "Mother Church of Country Music," the Ryman Auditorium was built by riverboat captain and saloon owner, Thomas Ryman (no relation to Tennessee minimalist painter Robert Ryman). Originally called the Union Gospel Tabernacle, it was renamed for Ryman after his death.

The tabernacle served as a church for Sam P. Jones, the revivalist preacher who converted Ryman to the Christian faith. It also served as the home of Trevecca Nazarene University from 1911 to 1914, before famously becoming the home of the

Grand Ole Opry from 1943 until 1974. When the Opry moved its show to a newly built venue in the Opryland theme park, the building fell into disrepair until 1992, when country star Emmylou Harris recorded her *Live at the Ryman* album in the space. The record created a new interest in the building, and the Ryman Auditorium reopened—newly restored—in 1994. Today, the Ryman is a museum and a live performance venue where patrons still sit in the pews just like they did in 1891.

Graceland

Originally owned by Memphis newspaper publisher S.E. Toof, Graceland was named after Toof's daughter, Grace. Toof's niece, Ruth Moore, and her husband built the home at Graceland in 1939. Elvis Presley bought Graceland in 1957 in order to have more security and privacy as his celebrity grew. The mansion is famous for Elvis' eclectic remodeling and decorating. The infamous "Jungle Room" featured a cascading waterfall before being converted into Elvis' last recording studio in 1976.

Graceland is nearly twice as big as it was when Elvis originally purchased it, and one of the best-known additions is the Meditation Gardens, where Elvis' mother, father, grandmother, twin brother and the King himself—who died at the home in 1976—are all buried.

FAMOUS TENNESSEE LANDMARKS

Montgomery Bell Tunnel

In the city of White Bluff, what might look to be some sort of natural wonder is actually a marvel of construction. The Montgomery Bell Tunnel was commissioned by the man for whom it was named. Bell was a manufacturer and an entrepreneur who was instrumental in the early development of Middle Tennessee. His greatest project was the creation of a 200-foot-long tunnel through a limestone ridge on the Harpeth River in 1819. The entire tunnel was built by slaves who used hand tools and black powder to blast through the limestone. Bell's masterpiece was the first full-scale water-diversion tunnel in the U.S., and the resulting water supply powered Bell's iron mill, which was very successful and added to Bell's reputation as the "Iron Master of Middle Tennessee."

A Real Gem

At 145 feet in height, Ruby Falls is the highest underground waterfall in the world. Located 1120 feet beneath the surface of Lookout Mountain, Ruby Falls sits at the heart of the Ruby Cave. The cave is a limestone structure formed through natural erosion by water. In the past, when the water level in the area was higher, rushing currents washed out the cave and enlarged other channels and cracks beneath the mountain. After the cave was formed, another stream entered from the surface, ultimately causing a sinkhole that let in massive amounts of water. The hollowed-out dome at the top of the cave was created by the falls and is also known as Solomon's Temple.

The Lost Sea

As the largest underground lake in America, the Lost Sea's reputation is certified by the *Guinness Book of Records*. Part of an ancient, extensive system of caves known as the Craighead Caverns, the Lost Sea was discovered in 1905 by a 13-year-old boy named Ben Sands. The boy reported that the room containing the lake was so big that even when he threw mud balls into the dark as hard as he could, he heard nothing but splashes all around him. Still a mystery, the total size of the lake—which descends into deeper subterranean caverns—has resisted measurement, even with trained divers and modern equipment.

More than 13 acres of the lake have been documented so far, but no end has yet been found. The lake plays host to some of the largest rainbow trout in the North America, though fishing is strictly prohibited.

Stairway to Heaven
The Appalachian Trail, a popular hiking route, winds for 371 miles through East Tennessee and along the Tennessee–North Carolina border, creating a greenway that connects 14 different states. The "AT," as it's known, passes through the Great Smoky Mountains National Park and the highest point on the entire trail is at Clingman's Dome. Measuring 6643 feet tall, Clingman's Dome is also the highest point in Tennessee and the country's second highest geographic elevation east of the Mississippi River. This stretch of the Appalachian Trail is understood to be one of the most dangerous because of the high elevations and the sudden weather changes that are common in the area. Lightning is a regular threat during the summer months, and freak snowstorms have stranded hikers even in April and May.

Legendary Lake

According to a Chickasaw Indian legend, Reelfoot Lake was formed when the gods opened up the earth to swallow a tribe that had stolen Starlight, a Choctaw princess, for their chief to marry. The lake is located in northwestern Tennessee and extends into Fulton County, Kentucky. According to science, the lake was formed by earthquakes that shook the area in 1811 and 1812. Accounts of the quake describe the Mississippi River flowing backwards, its waters rising high enough to submerge trees along the 30-foot-high bank. After the most violent quake on February 16, 1812, reports of a new lake began to circulate. Today, the lake is known for its outstanding fishing, its bald cypress trees and its population of bald eagles—apparently, they know about the great fishing, too!

A Long Way Down

One of the highest waterfalls east of the Rocky Mountains, Fall Creek Falls thunders down a full 256 feet. The falls are located in Fall Creek Falls State Park, between Spencer and Pikeville in Middle Tennessee. The artificial Fall Creek Falls Lake is controlled by a dam that ensures a constant flow of water over the falls. One of the most beautiful natural areas in the state, the park was a primary location for Disney's live-action version of *The Jungle Book*, as well as the 1995 film *Mighty Morphin' Power Rangers: The Movie*.

ROADSIDE ATTRACTIONS

Bell Witch Cave

The legend of the Bell Witch is not only Tennessee's most famous ghost story—it's quite likely the most popular supernatural tale in the country. Simply put, a woman named Kate Batts believed she was being cheated by a man named John Bell when she bought some land from him. Before Kate Batts drew her last breath, she promised to return to haunt Bell and his descendants, which, according to Bell's daughter Betsy, she's done quite successfully. The Bell farm and a cave located nearby were preserved, and today tours of the area are possible, though by appointment only. The Bell Witch Cave is located near Adams.

Bigger...Always Better?

A three-story, 70-foot-long guitar built in 1983 by Joe Morrell as an advertising gimmick for his museum in Bristol has become a favorite spot for tourists to stop and pose for a photo. Morrell's Grand Guitar Museum is now closed, but the guitar that Morrell built has made its way into "Believe It or Not" fame.

DID YOU KNOW?

The most popular park in the U.S. federal park system is the Great Smoky Mountains National Park, located in East Tennessee. According to its official website, the park hosts as many as 10,000,000 people each year.

One For the Weird Files

PETA enthusiasts would have had a coronary had they been around in 1916 when, in an effort to deal with an Asian elephant that had a particularly brutal reputation, the authorities decided to hang the animal. The poor beast didn't die after the first effort, but was horribly injured. The second time, she was strung up by a crane attached to a rail car at the Clinchfield

Yards, and this time she mercifully perished. Her story has been told throughout the years, and newspaper clippings reporting her "execution" are on display at the Unicoi County Heritage Museum.

One and Only

Gatlinburg is home to the world's only Salt and Pepper Shaker Museum. The museum boasts more than 20,000 salt and pepper shakers from all over the world.

Furry and White

Kenton is just one of five U.S. communities that claim to be the "White Squirrel Capital of the World." Although the communities may be challenging each other for the title, it's a fact that if you visit Kenton, you're fairly likely to catch a glimpse of one of the more than 200 albino squirrels living in the area.

Crystal Shrine Grotto

The life of Jesus is laid out in a series of 10 scenes carved into an artificial cave in the Memorial Park Cemetery in Memphis. The art, created by Dionicio Rodriquez, took more than 10 years to complete. Rodriquez began the creation of what's now known as the Crystal Shrine Grotto in 1937.

City of Secrets

Oak Ridge has branded itself as the "Energy Capital of the World," but when the city was first established in 1940, it kept that—along with the fact that the city even existed—to itself. You see, the "secret city" was created as a scientific research facility and was instrumental in the development of the atomic bomb.

TENNESSEE TIDBIT Virginia was the only state in the country that saw more Civil War battles than Tennessee. To commemorate Tennessee's involvement, four national military parks have been established in the state at Chickamauga-Chattanooga, Stones River, Shiloh and Fort Donelson.

TENNESSEE'S TOP TEAMS

The Tennessee Titans

Tennessee's first-ever pro football team, the Tennessee Titans started out as the Houston Oilers professional football franchise in 1960. The team had an auspicious start, winning the first two AFL Championships in 1960 and 1961 before the league merged with the NFL in 1970. The team enjoyed some success in the late 1970s but mostly struggled for decades before moving to Nashville in 1997, where they spent three years as the Tennessee Oilers. Changing their name to the Titans and moving into Nashville's new Adelphia Coliseum in 1999 brought new life to the team. They ended that season with a heartbreaking 23–16 loss to the St. Louis Rams in Super Bowl XXXIV. The Titans have gone on to win Division Championships in 2000, 2002 and 2008. Since moving to Tennessee, the team has made the playoffs six out of its 12 years in the state.

In the 2009 movie *Moon*, Sam Rockwell's character has a Tennessee Titans poster in his bedroom at the lunar base.

Cats on Ice

Tennessee's first-ever professional hockey team, the Nashville Predators belong to the Central Division of the NHL's Western Conference. While we don't usually associate hockey with warm, southern states, Tennessee first hosted the Nashville Dixie Flyers of the Eastern Hockey League in 1962. After several minor league teams and a possible relocation by the New Jersey Devils fueled hockey rumors in Music City, the Predators expansion team finally hit the home ice in 1998. By 2007, rumors of a possible sale of the team had the Predators potentially moving to Ontario, Canada, or to Kansas City, Kansas, but a group of local business owners—Our Team Nashville—stepped up to keep the team in Nashville. Barry Trotz has been the team's head coach for their entire history. After their first 10 seasons, the Predators had posted a record 364 wins and 342 losses.

DID YOU  KNOW?

"Gnash," the Predator's mascot, is a saber-toothed tiger. The chomping cheerleader is a reference to an actual *Smilodon floridanus* skeleton that was unearthed in downtown Nashville during a building project in 1971. This is only the fifth skeleton of its kind to be discovered in North America.

For the Love of the Game

Even though Tennessee doesn't have a professional baseball team to root for, their love for "America's pastime" is evident in the plethora of minor league teams that thrive around the state:

- Memphis Redbirds
- Nashville Sounds
- Tennessee Smokies
- West Tennessee Diamond Jaxx
- Chattanooga Lookouts
- Elizabethton Twins
- Johnson City Cardinals
- Kingsport Mets
- Greenville Astros

DID YOU  KNOW?

Music legends Bob Dylan and Willie Nelson have scheduled several summer concert tours booked exclusively at minor league baseball parks all over America.

The Big Orange

The Volunteers of the University of Tennessee (UT) carry on a proud athletic tradition at their Knoxville campus, and, on any given Saturday afternoon during the NCAA football season, it can sometimes seem like the entire state must have turned the team's well-known hue of deep orange. As a Division I-A member of the Southeastern Conference (SEC), the Volunteers compete in 20 varsity intercollegiate sports, including football, basketball, swimming, diving, tennis and more.

Always a tough competitor in the SEC, UT's athletic program has claimed a number of honors, awards and milestones that have made the Volunteers' tradition one of the most admired in the South:

- ☞ The Volunteer's football team has won six NCAA National Championships and 13 SEC Championships.

- ☞ Since 2000, the Volunteers have had 10 players awarded First Team positions as NCAA All-Americans and 33 players named All-SEC.

- ☞ Since 2000, the Volunteers have seen 10 former players go on to be picked as first-round draft choices in the NFL, and standout former Volunteers like Al Wilson (Denver Broncos), Jason Witten (Dallas Cowboys), Albert Haynesworth (Tennessee Titans) and Peyton Manning (Indianapolis Colts) have appeared regularly in the NFL Pro Bowl during the past decade.

- Under the leadership of Pat Summit, the Lady Volunteers basketball team has become the greatest women's basketball dynasty in the history of the NCAA.

- Pat Summit is the most successful basketball coach in NCAA history—including men's sports and all divisions—and she is one of only three basketball coaches to have attained the milestone of 1000 wins.

- Between 1987 and 2008, the Lady Volunteers basketball team won eight division championships, the most in the history of women's basketball. The team's undefeated season and National Championship in 1998 was documented in Pat Summit's book *Raise the Roof*.

Tiger Tales

Clad in their traditional blue and gray, the Tigers of the University of Memphis play every game according to one of the school's oldest athletic mottoes: "Every Man a Tiger!" The Tigers suit up both men's and women's teams in nine sports, representing Memphis in NCAA Division I as members of Conference USA. Recent decades have seen the Tigers' men's basketball and football programs attracting controversy and success alike:

WELCOME TO TENNESSEE

- The Memphis Tigers' men's basketball program first found the national spotlight in 1973 when the team competed with UCLA Bruins for the NCAA Division I Championship.

- The basketball squad continued to excel in the '80s and made it to the Final Four before losing to Villanova. The Tigers went to the Elite Eight in the NCAA Championships in 2006, 2007 and 2008, and their record between 2005 and 2009 was a staggering 137–14. The Tigers were undefeated during the regular season in 2007.

- The Tigers' trip to the 1985 Final Four had to be canceled after the NCAA found coach Dana Kirk and his staff guilty of a number of recruiting violations. Eventually, evidence surfaced that Kirk was guilty of scalping tickets, soliciting kickbacks from sponsors and facilitating the payment of players by boosters. Kirk eventually spent four months in a federal minimum-security prison in Montgomery, Alabama. Although Kirk built the Tigers into a national phenomenon using mostly Memphis-area players, he only graduated six student-athletes in seven years at the school.

- The Tigers' football program dates back to 1912. They currently call the 62,380-seat Liberty Bowl Memorial Stadium home, and they played in five bowl games during six seasons from 2003 to 2008.

- The Tigers' football team was led to the Motor City Bowl by their All-American running back DeAngelo Williams in 2005. Williams went on to become a first-round draft pick for the Carolina Panthers of the NFL.

Go Commodores!

The only private school in the SEC, Vanderbilt University's Commodores are a charter member of the conference, and they field 16 men's and women's teams in the NCAA's Division I. Participating in sports that include football, basketball, swimming and lacrosse, the Commodores take their moniker from a nickname that was earned by Cornelius Vanderbilt for his success as a shipping magnate. The Vanderbilt University campus in Nashville is home to the 40,200-seat Vanderbilt Stadium.

☛ The Commodores' main rivalry is with their cross-state opponents, the University of Tennessee Volunteers.

WELCOME TO TENNESSEE

- Most Vanderbilt fans cheer their team on with the simple cry of "Go 'Dores!" and the school's Commodore mascot is a 19th-century naval officer with bushy sideburns, naval regalia and a cutlass-style sword at the ready.

- A private school with a well-known academic and research reputation, Vanderbilt's sports teams have always had a tough go in the super-competitive SEC, but the school's fight song "Dynamite" extols the virtues of playing hard and cheering with enthusiasm whether the team wins or loses.

- In the 21st century, the Commodores baseball team has done especially well, making the NCAA Super Regionals in 2004 and winning both the SEC regular season and SEC tournament crowns in 2007.

- During the 2008 season, the Commodores football team posted a winning record and proved eligible for a bowl game, a feat they hadn't accomplished in 53 years. The Commodores beat the Boston College Eagles in a dramatic come-from-behind victory in the Music City Bowl on December 31, 2008—the final score was 16–14.

 The name of Vanderbilt University's marching band is the Spirit of Gold Marching Band.

WELCOME TO TENNESSEE

TENNESSEE SCHOOLS' REPORT CARD

In 1913, Tennessee became the first among the southern states to enact compulsory school attendance. By 1923, the Tennessee Department of Education was established. In 1947, the state's first sales tax was levied, and 80 percent of the tax proceeds went to supporting the public school system. Tennessee continues to be a leader in education in the Southeast. In 1984, the state enacted the Better Schools Program of educational reform, and in 1992, the Education Improvement Act renewed the state's position as a national education leader.

By the Numbers

According to the Tennessee Department of Education's Report Card for 2009:

- Tennessee is home to 1736 schools serving grades PK to 12.

- Over 930,500 students are served in Tennessee by 63,765 teachers and 4314 administrators.

- All of Tennessee's schools are "safe" according to the Report Card's Safe School Status.

- Student racial diversity statistics find 664,138 Caucasian students, 239,163 African Americans, 50,652 Hispanics, 15,925 Asian-Pacific Islanders and 2064 Asians.

- Tennessee's public schools claim 33,673 limited-English proficient students, 134,932 students with disabilities and 529,467 students from economically disadvantaged homes.

- The male to female student ratio is nearly one-to-one, at 499,815 to 472,127, respectively.

- Average achievement on the ACT test has increased between 2007 and 2009.

- Attendance-promotion rates have both increased since 2007—currently, Tennessee boasts a 95.2 percent rate of attendance and a 98.5 percent rate of promotion.

- Tennessee has a state goal of 90 percent as a graduation rate; currently, the state graduates 82.2 percent.

- According to figures collected by the state of Tennessee, 69.3 percent of adults have a high school diploma (or equivalent) or better and 9.3 percent of adults have a bachelor's degree or better.

TENNESSEE COLLEGES AND UNIVERSITIES

Tennessee is home to a diverse range of colleges and universities, from well-known research institutions such as Vanderbilt to technological schools like Tennessee Tech. The state is home to private schools like the University of the South, as well as nationally recognized state colleges like the University of Tennessee. The city of Nashville is known as the "Athens of the South" for its plethora of opportunities for higher learning, and the entire state plays host to students from near and far who are seeking out the challenges and benefits of a dynamic, engaging educational experience. The following list is not comprehensive, but it does offer a profile of the diverse academic experiences that await students in the Volunteer State.

WELCOME TO TENNESSEE

Vanderbilt University

Located just outside downtown Nashville, Vanderbilt University was established in 1873 as a gift from shipping magnate Cornelius Vanderbilt. Its reputation as a top-flight academic institution has always attracted the cream of the crop from the rest of the nation's high schools, and its well-known law, medicine and divinity programs are all in-demand graduate programs that draw students from around the world. Vanderbilt currently hosts students from all 50 states and 90 different countries. Vanderbilt boasts a nine-to-one student-to-faculty ratio, and nearly all the undergraduate classes are taught by senior, tenured professors. Vanderbilt's meandering campus encompasses 330 acres, and its tree-covered grounds are recognized as a national arboretum featuring over 300 species of trees.

In addition to the university itself, Vanderbilt is also affiliated with a number of additional institutes and research facilities, including the Vanderbilt Institute for Public Policy Studies, Freedom Forum First Amendment Center, Dyer Observatory and the Vanderbilt University Medical Center, Middle Tennessee's only level 1 trauma center.

DID YOU KNOW?

Vanderbilt University claims several distinguished alumni, including author Robert Penn Warren, former U.S. senator and actor Fred Thompson, singer Amy Grant and both Al and Tipper Gore.

 Tusculum College is Tennessee's oldest college. It is located in Greene County.

WELCOME TO TENNESSEE

Sewanee, the University of the South

Often referred to simply as "Sewanee," the University of the South is located on 13,000 acres of picturesque mountain property on the Cumberland Plateau, just north of Chattanooga. Sewanee is a private liberal arts college owned by 28 separate dioceses of the Episcopal Church. The university's School of Theology is an official Episcopal Seminary. Founded on July 4, 1857, the school's cornerstone was laid at the top of Monteagle Mountain on October 10, 1860. Construction of the university was interrupted by fighting during the Civil War, and the existing structures were partially destroyed by Union soldiers in 1863. Renowned for its academic traditions, Sewanee is particularly known for its literary excellence, and the school currently offers masters degrees in American literature and creative writing.

Sewanee's sports mascot is the tiger, and the University of the South competes in 11 men's and 13 women's sports as part of the Southern Collegiate Athletic Conference in Division III of the NCAA. Boasting over 12,000 alumni from 50 states and 40 countries, Sewanee has produced 25 Rhodes scholars and dozens of Fulbright scholarship winners. Alumni of the School of Theology include three of the last five presiding bishops of the Episcopal Church.

In 1983, Tennessee Williams left his literary rights to the university. Royalties from the Pulitzer Prize–winner's works have assisted in the construction of the college's Tennessee Williams Center performance venue.

Union University

Located in Jackson, about 80 miles east of Memphis, Union University was established in 1823 and is the oldest school associated with the Southern Baptist Convention. A private, four-year liberal arts university, Union offers bachelor's, master's and doctoral degree programs in disciplines ranging from art to nursing to business administration and Christian studies. The university strives to produce alumni that are "excellence-driven, Christ-centered, people-focused and future-directed." Serving a small student body, Union hosts about 4000 undergrad and graduate students from 40 states and 35 different countries. The university boasts a 12-to-one student-to-faculty ratio, and 83 percent of the faculty hold the highest degree possible in their field of expertise.

DID YOU KNOW?

Union University is a conglomeration of a few older institutions: the West Tennessee College, its predecessor, as well as the Jackson Male Academy and Union University of Murfreesboro.

Rhodes College

Located on 100-acre plot within a historic neighborhood near downtown Memphis, Rhodes College offers an idyllic learning environment right in the heart of Tennessee's largest urban center. Established in 1948, Rhodes currently enrolls nearly 2000 students from 46 states and 15 foreign countries. The student-to-faculty ratio at Rhodes College is 10 to one, with biology, history, English, business and psychology being the most popular courses of study. Rhodes graduates are twice as likely to be accepted into medical schools, and the college boasts a 95 percent placement rate for its grads that apply to business, divinity and law schools. The school's athletic mascot is the lynx, and Rhodes teams compete in the Southern Collegiate Athletic Conference in Division III of the NCAA.

DID YOU KNOW?

Rhodes College traces its lineage back to an earlier institution—the Southwestern Presbyterian University. The college adopted its current name in 1984 in honor of Peyton Nalle Rhodes, the institution's former president.

Fisk University

A historically black university in Nashville, Fisk University was founded in 1866. The Fisk Free Colored School was established only six months after the end of the Civil War. The school's mission was to educate newly liberated freemen, and enrollment jumped to nearly 1000 students only months after the institution began operations.

Clinton B. Fisk—the university's namesake—supplied the fledgling school with an endowment of $30,000. In 1930, Fisk became the very first African American school to be awarded accreditation by the Southern Association of Colleges and Schools. Fisk was also the first largely black college to gain a Phi Beta Kappa charter, which inducted its first members in 1953. In 2008, Nashville's Metro Council declared March 19 to be Fisk University Day. The Fisk Bulldogs athletic teams wear gold and blue, and the school's famous Fisk Jubilee Singers are known around the world.

In 1946, American painter Georgia O'Keeffe gifted Fisk University with 101 paintings, sculptures, prints and photographs from the estate of her deceased husband, photographer Alfred Stieglitz. The Stieglitz Collection now includes works by 29 American and European artists, including Pablo Picasso, Paul Cezanne, Pierre-Auguste Renoir, Diego Rivera, Arthur Dove, Henri de Toulouse-Lautrec and, of course, Georgia O'Keeffe.

The Fisk Jubilee Singers introduced Negro spirituals (slave songs) to the world in 1871. In 2000, the singers were featured in *Jubilee*

Singers: Sacrifice and Glory, a documentary that aired as part of the award-winning PBS series *American Experience*.

The University of Tennessee
Founded in 1794, the University of Tennessee (UT) underwent a few transformations before becoming the school we know and love today. Beginning its life as Blount College, the institution changed its name to East Tennessee College in 1807 and became East Tennessee University in 1840. The school was awarded a land grant in 1869 and became the University of Tennessee in 1879. The university is accredited by the Commission on Colleges of the Southern Association of Colleges and Schools, and it awards bachelor's, master's and doctoral degrees. The University's main campus is located in Knoxville, where the rambling grounds afford picturesque vistas of the Great Smoky Mountains National Park.

Known for its nationally recognized sports teams as well as its top-flight research, UT co-manages the Oak Ridge National Laboratory, offering students unparalleled access to the Department of Energy's largest science and energy laboratory. The University of Tennessee is the state's best-known institution of higher learning, and it has a reputation as one of the top public research facilities in the nation. UT currently enrolls nearly 30,000 students and offers 300 degree programs.

In addition to its main Knoxville campus, the University of Tennessee operates satellite campuses around the state in Chattanooga, Martin, Tullahoma and Memphis. The campus in Tullahoma is also a space institute.

Middle Tennessee State University
Founded as a state-run normal school for training teachers in 1911, Middle Tennessee State University (MTSU) became the State Teachers College in 1925, offering a bachelor of science degree—a bachelor of arts degree was added in 1936.

The institution's name was changed to State College in 1943, and it added a graduate school in 1951. It finally achieved university status in 1965. Currently, MTSU boasts a 504-acre campus located in Murfreesboro—close to the exact geographic center of the Tennessee. MTSU includes seven university colleges, and it offers eight bachelor's degrees in arts, business administration, fine arts, music, science, social work, science in nursing and university studies. The school's graduate degree programs offer 10 master's degrees, as well as doctorate level degrees in art and philosophy. MTSU's athletic teams, the Blue Raiders, compete in the Sun Belt Conference.

DID YOU  KNOW?

The Blue Raider's team name is credited to Charles Sarver. In 1934, Sayer won five dollars in an official Murfreesboro *Daily News Journal* contest to name the team. For years, the Blue Raiders were represented by Ole Blue—a cartoon dog that resembled a bluetick hound. In 1998, the team adopted their new mascot, Lightning—a winged horse borrowed from Greek mythology.

Tennessee Technological University

The *Princeton Review* recognizes Tennessee Tech as one of the best learning institutions in the Southeast, and such recognition is especially sweet given that the school literally began as a grassroots effort by handful of Cookeville community leaders to create a center for higher learning in what was little more than a field of daisies located in Tennessee's Upper Cumberland region.

In 1909, the University of Dixie—as it was originally named—began classes at the high school and junior college levels despite having a low enrollment and financial instability. By 1929, Dixie graduated its first four-year bachelor degree students, and by 1949, the population and enrollment booms that followed World War II allowed the institution to expand into five separate schools: Agriculture and Home Economics, Arts and Sciences, Business Administration, Education and Engineering.

In 1965, the Tennessee Technological Institute was awarded university status, becoming Tennessee Technological University. The little daisy field where the school began has now expanded into an 87-building complex that sprawls across 235 acres. Tennessee Tech's current enrollment exceeds 10,000 students, and the university employs 370 faculty members. The school offers a variety of programs from high school diploma preparation to doctoral degrees in education, engineering and environmental sciences.

TENNESSEE TIDBIT Tennessee Technological University alumni Barry Wilmore was the pilot of the final space shuttle mission that launched on November 16, 2009. Wilmore graduated with electrical engineering degrees in 1985 and 1994.

WHAT'S IN A NAME?

Bucksnort

A small, unincorporated community in Hickman County, Bucksnort is located along the I-40 just east of the Tennessee River. Known to some people as the home of professional wrestler "Dirty" Dutch Mantel, the tiny spot is probably best known for its rather abrupt place name.

The name's tale is somewhat confusing, as the original town of Bucksnort was actually in Lincoln County—that community later became known as Mimosa in 1898, but the legend of the Bucksnort name still holds. Apparently, William "Buck" Pamplin owned land in the area. Pamplin, you see, loved whiskey, and when he'd had his fill of the good stuff, his laugh would be reduced to a loud, snorting sound that was recognized throughout the county. The rest, as they say, is history. Nowadays, the town's name still attracts tourists, and it is also known for its family fishing at the Bucksnort Trout Ranch fish farm.

Gilt Edge

Gilt Edge is a city of less than 500 in Tipton County on the state's southwest border. Opinions differ regarding the origin of this place name—some say Gilt Edge was named after a well-known brand of shoe polish; others say the town took its name as a commitment to an affluent future. It seems like the latter may be the more likely explanation—recent numbers show that the median household income in the tiny town cashes in at $46,250, as compared to the national average of $41,994.

Liepers Fork

This oddly named community is not really known for its utensil making or for its long-distance jumping. Liepers Fork is an unincorporated community located in Williamson County. The area was originally settled by explorers from Virginia and North Carolina in the 1790s, and the community's odd name comes from one of these original settlers. It seems that Mr. Lieper discovered a fork in the local creek and the name just stuck. This same Mr. Lieper was later killed by Native Americans, but the community has survived just fine.

Leipers Fork is on the National Register of Historic Places because of its many examples of 19th-century architecture. The area is also known for its history as a moonshine whiskey center, and it's said that the remains of old whiskey stills can still be found in the local woods.

Nameless

Nameless is an unincorporated community in Jackson County. Although there is no agreement regarding the origin of the "name" of Nameless, the possible explanations are almost as interesting as this nearly anonymous place name.

One version about the name's origin claims that early community leaders inadvertently left a blank space on their application for a U.S. post office. When the application was returned, the community was simply referred to as Nameless. In another version, the town was to be named Morgan, but federal authorities balked at the request, feeling that the Morgan name was a tribute to Confederate Army General John Hunt Morgan. When the name was rejected, the stubborn people of "Nameless" were all too happy to do without a proper designation.

DID YOU KNOW?

Singer-songwriter Elvis Costello mentions Nameless in his song "My Dark Life."

Paris

Paris is the oldest incorporated municipality in the state. Located in Henry County, the city's name has a history that reaches all the way back to the American Revolution.

When the town was founded, county commissioner James Leeper suggested that the community be called Lafayette in honor of the Marquis de Lafayette, the Frenchman who had been such a great help to the American military during the war. As luck would have it, Lafayette was also the name that ended up being pulled from a hat at random when all the various suggestions were pooled. However, not everyone was as crazy for the name as Mr. Leeper was. Fearing that most citizens would misspell the name, they all compromised and Paris,

Tennessee, was born. Today, Paris is known for its 60-foot-tall replica of the Eiffel Tower and for an annual spring celebration that is touted as the "World's Biggest Fish Fry."

Red Boiling Springs

During the 1830s, a Kentucky hunter named Edmund Jennings was one of the first pioneers to find his way into this lovely valley. After hearing stories about the beautiful land, Shepherd Kirby became one of the first settlers to move his family to the area. Kirby suffered from painful eye infections and had put up with the misery for years. One day, the pain was especially unbearable, and out of desperation, he washed his eyes in a nearby spring. To his astonishment, his condition was greatly improved the next day. Kirby continued his trips to the spring until his condition was completely cured. Soon, other people started flocking to the area seeking their own cures from the healing spring waters that bubbled up from the ground with a telltale reddish tint. Today, the city of Red Boiling Springs has a little over 1000 residents—the entire city is just under 1.5 square miles and is located in Macon County.

Skullbone

Although this cranial place name doesn't appear on every map of the state, you can rest assured that there really is a Skullbone, Tennessee. Located on SR-105 between Trezvant and Bradford, this small community may not be very big, but you better believe it packs a punch. In its wilder days, Skullbone became famous—or rather, infamous—for staging knockdown, drag-out, bare-knuckle boxing matches. The one rule was that you could only strike your opponent above the shoulders. Today, the town celebrates its bruised and battered past by selling every kind of skull-decorated novelty memorabilia you can imagine.

ORIGINS OF TENNESSEE COUNTIES

Like the entire state of Tennessee, each of its counties has a unique history, punctuated by tales of adventure, hardship, struggles lost and victories won. Here are a few of their stories.

Franklin County

Franklin County was created in 1807 after Rutherford County was combined with Native American lands. The county was named in honor of the painter, diplomat, author, philosopher, scientist and statesman, Benjamin Franklin. The name was also a remnant of the failed state of Franklin that preceded the state of Tennessee.

The creation of the county caused an influx of settlers from East Tennessee, Virginia and North Carolina. The city of Winchester—Franklin's county seat—is named for General James Winchester. Primarily an agricultural farming region, Franklin County farmers grew cotton, which they floated down the Elk River to markets in New Orleans. However, like the rest of the state, crops such as corn and wheat thrived along with livestock. The county was greatly impacted by the building of the Nashville and Chattanooga Railroad in 1854—the railroad lines quickly expanded to accommodate more mining in the area. Franklin County was a hotbed of secessionist sentiment, and a regiment from the area pledged to serve with the rebels before Tennessee officially left the Union.

After the Civil War, the area was again transformed by burgeoning African American communities. Agriculture was slow to recover, but the Swiss and German immigrants in Belvedere led the way back to productivity with their Old World persistence and their distinctive, round barns. The army training facility of Camp Forrest was established near the county's northern border during World War II—after the war, the camp became the Arnold Engineering Development Center, an air force aerospace testing facility. The center's need for water led to the Tennessee Valley Authority's damming of the Elk River, creating the Woods Reservoir with the Tims Ford Dam.

Grainger County

Grainger County was created in 1796 and named in honor of Mary Grainger—the only county in Tennessee named after a woman. The daughter of Kaleb Grainger of North Carolina, Mary wed William Blount and became the first lady of the Territory South of the River Ohio (later renamed Tennessee). Still largely rural, Grainger sits between the Holston and Clinch rivers, and the county seat of Rutledge has approximately 2500 residents.

Agriculture has always been a mainstay in the area—tobacco and cattle are the major products grown in the area, and Grainger County tomatoes are known and enjoyed nationwide. In its early days, small businesses catered to travelers on the New Orleans to Washington road—hat stores, saddle makers, dry goods merchants, hotels and taverns all thrived on tourist dollars and supplied goods to nearby rural communities. A flourishing spa economy developed around the area's mineral springs until the Great Depression, but the TVA's construction of Cherokee Lake to the south of the county and Norris Lake to the north have created a flourishing recreation industry that provides fishing, camping, boating and a lake-front property market.

DID YOU KNOW?

A number of notable citizens come from Grainger County, most famously the Cocke family, which had several family members who served in state and national legislatures, including John Cocke (1796–1801, 1807–13 and 1843–45), William Cocke (1813–15), Sterling Cocke (1815–19) and William Michael Cocke (1855–57).

Lake County

The aqueous appellation of this county comes from Reelfoot Lake, which was created by an earthquake in 1811. Nestled in the northwest corner of the state, Lake County is bounded by Kentucky to the north, Reelfoot Lake to the east and the Mississippi River to the west. Encompassing 210 square miles, this flatland county has some of the most fertile soil in Tennessee. Although legends persist that the lake was named after a Native American chief, it's more likely that it was named for Bill Jones, an early resident whose clubfoot earned him the appellation "Reelfoot Jones." Jones died after he slipped and drowned in Spring Creek in March 1839. The creek was given the nickname "Reelfoot Creek," and the shallow lake it fed into soon acquired the moniker as well. The county was first organized in 1870, and Tiptonville was named its county seat.

Because of its treasured soil, the area has a long agricultural history. Cotton and soybeans have always thrived in the area, and there are families in the county who have held plots of farmland for generations. When the Illinois Central Railroad was established, cotton mills sprang up along the tracks to process cotton for distant markets—a cotton gin still operates in the county today. During the early 1900s, the West Tennessee Land Company took control of Reelfoot Lake and attempted to drain it for cotton production. Residents rebelled, and the ensuing conflict resulted in the death of a company attorney and the arrest of nearly 300 citizens who were accused of staging night raids to terrorize the company and its supporters. Eventually, all charges were dropped against the supposed raiders, and the control of Reelfoot Lake fell to the state, which opened it to public use in 1914.

DID YOU KNOW?

Tiptonville is the early home of rock 'n' roll pioneer Carl Perkins. Perkins was an architect of the rockabilly guitar style and the writer of the famous song "Blue Suede Shoes."

Lawrence County

Lawrence County was created in 1817 after Native American lands were combined with Hickman County. The area was named for James Lawrence, an American naval officer who was killed while commanding the *Chesapeake* against the British frigate *Shannon*. Lawrence is also famous for his dying words: "Don't give up the ship!"

The seat of the county is located in Lawrenceburg, and a number of smaller communities developed around the iron ore mines in the county. The area attracted many waves of migration from all over the Carolinas and the Deep South but is notable for two more "exotic" arrivals.

In the early 1870s, a large number of German Catholic immigrants settled in communities like Loretto and St. Joseph, bringing many skilled tradesmen into the local economies. Then, in 1944, a large contingent of Amish citizens settled in and around Ethridge. Their farming, handicrafts and simple lifestyle won them a permanent place in the county. Around this same time, the Murray Ohio Manufacturing Company moved to Lawrence County. The company created 3000 jobs in the area, putting its citizens to work building a wide range of items, from bikes and lawnmowers to countertops and fishing lures. The county is now home to nearly 40,000 Tennesseans. Actor, former U.S. senator and presidential candidate Fred Thompson hails from Lawrenceburg.

DID YOU KNOW?

Tennessee legend Davy Crockett called Lawrenceburg home for a time, and he served as one of its first county commissioners. Crockett operated a number of businesses in the area, including a distillery. The site of his former home is now the David Crockett State Park, where every year tourists flock for the annual David Crockett Days celebration.

Lewis County

Created in 1843 from Hickman, Lawrence, Maury and Wayne counties, this locale was named for the great American explorer Meriwether Lewis. Although a county seat has been established more than once, the current seat of Hohenwald was settled on in 1923. Although some farming is done in the area, the county's soil is not very agriculture-friendly, and the region instead became a center for iron-ore mining, pig-iron production, cotton growing and the manufacturing of cotton yarn.

By the end of the Civil War, all the industry had been closed and the farmlands had suffered nearly irreparable losses. It took an influx of German and Swiss citizens—*hohenwald* is Swiss for "high forest"—to breathe new life into the community in the late-19th century. European music, waltzes at Hohenwald Society Park and German- and Swiss-language churches flourished until anti-German sentiments eroded these traditions during World War II. Today, Lewis County enjoys a diverse economy and has a population of just over 11,000 and rising.

DID YOU  KNOW?

Meriweather Lewis—the county's namesake—was buried at Grinder's Stand in Lewis County in 1809. To this day, it is still a mystery whether his death was a murder or a suicide.

Loudon County

Created in 1870 from a blending of Roane, Monroe, Blount and McMinn counties, the county was named for Fort Loudon, which was erected in 1756 by the British and named after the French and Indian War commander-in-chief, the Earl of Loudon. Major William B. Lenoir, an early founder of the area, developed a successful plantation that became known for its hog and cattle farming. Lenoir and his family also established cotton and flour mills in the area, and the town of Lenoir is named after the family. A hosiery industry was established in the town of Philadelphia in 1821, and the industry flourished well into the 1870s.

After the Civil War, the county slowly rebuilt a manufacturing base, and the Bass Foundry and Machine Shop became an important employer, building railroad cars for the Southern Railroad Company as the Lenoir Car Works. TVA projects on the area's rivers also transformed Loudon County—the building of the Fort Loudon Dam in the 1940s and the Tellico Dam in the 1970s created Tellico Lake and the residential community of Tellico Village. Both added significantly to the local economy and the quality of life in the area. The county's population grew by 25 percent between 1990 and 2000.

Marion County

Marion County was named for Francis Marion, a military officer whose expertise as a guerrilla fighter during the Revolutionary War won him the nickname "Swamp Fox." Encompassing 500 square miles in the southern part of the Cumberland Plateau and the Sequatchie Valley, most of the area was occupied by Native tribes when the first white settlers arrived in the region. The tribes first had contact with outsiders in 1560, when Spanish soldiers from the expedition of Tristan de Luna entered the Tennessee River Valley and met with the Napochies tribe in what was then their main village. By the 1800s, this area was dominated by the Cherokee. Settlers signed a treaty to enter the valley in 1794 after Joseph Brown lead the famous Cumberland expedition that destroyed of the Native villages of Nickajack, Running Water and Long Island. Brown was acting out of vengeance for a Native ambush that resulted in the killing of his father and a number of other men in 1789. The women and children—Joseph Brown among them—were all captured. Brown soon escaped and clearly neither forgave nor forgot.

This zealous military tradition continued into the Civil War when the sorely divided county had sons from the same families separately joining both the Southern and the Northern armies. The railroads and turnpikes in the area helped the opposing factions crisscross the county, and their happenstance meetings often erupted in gunfire. After the war, the area prospered because of its mining and industry—coal and iron ore created a solid base for iron-making firms and other manufacturing companies. Today, the county is famous as a manufacturer of fireworks, and in 2000, it counted 27,776 citizens.

 One of Tennessee's oldest manufacturing firms, Lodge Cast Iron still operates out of the small town of South Pittsburgh. The long-lasting Lodge cookware is known around the world.

Obion County

Named for the Obion River, this county was created in 1823 from Indian lands—the etiology of the word "Obion" is a bit harder to track. One theory claims it is a Native American word meaning "many prongs," while another possibility is that Obion was the name of a Frenchman who first explored the area. Nestled in the rolling hills of northwest Tennessee, the county is known as the "Land of Green Pastures." It was settled by the Scots and the Irish by way of the Carolinas and Virginia. The first known white settler was a woman, Elisha Parker, who arrived in the area in 1819. Again, the ubiquitous Davy Crockett was present at the founding of this county as he was at so many others. Crockett served the area as a U.S. Congressman and holds a record hunting streak for killing 103 bears in the county. The present county seat of Union City came to prominence in 1854 when it became the location for the intersection of the Northwestern, Mobile and Ohio railroads. With a prosperous economy built around small farms growing tobacco, corn and wheat, the county added 12,800 residents in 1860 alone.

Following the Civil War, the county's recovery was hastened by the railroads, which made Union City into a commercial center, shipping a variety of products from the county's furniture manufacturers and sawmills to markets in the east. Nowadays, Union City is the site of a Tyson chicken processing plant that opened in 1996, and a former World War II aviation training field now serves as the Everett-Stewart Airport. The 2000 census listed the county's population at 32,450 citizens.

Sequatchie County

Created in 1857 from Hamilton, Marion and Warren counties, this county was named after the Cherokee chief whose name also graces the Sequatchie Valley. It is said that the name translates to "running or grinning opossum." The area has always been known for its agricultural richness, but it wasn't until the Anderson Pike was built in 1852 that farmers in the area really began to thrive. The road connected growers to the Western and Atlantic railroads in Atlanta, Georgia, and the area became well known for its livestock and its corn. As the railroads expanded further into the county, mining and lumber industries were established, and the Dunlap Coke Ovens became an important link to the burgeoning steel industry in the South at the turn of the century. However, the loss of these industries presaged the coming Great Depression, which hit this area harder than other parts of the state.

Raymond H. Cooley was a proud son of Dunlap before he became a staff sergeant, serving in the Pacific theater during World War II. Cooley won the Congressional Medal of Honor for his heroism during the invasion of the Philippines in 1945.

Union County

Created in 1850 from Grainger, Clairborne, Campbell, Anderson and Knox counties, the origin of the name of this county is unclear. While it is likely that the name simply reflects the hodge-podge makeup of the former counties under its new banner, it is also thought that the name was chosen to reflect the East Tennessee loyalty to the Federal Union. The county seat of Maynardville was named after brilliant young lawyer Horace Maynard, who successfully defended the creation of the county against furious opposition. The county wasn't officially created until 1856.

Union County was primarily an agricultural area, but tough conditions led to an exodus from the region. However, the Norris Dam project and the creation of the Norris reservoir created new opportunities and a number of new industries. In recent years, Union County has become a part of suburban Knoxville, and many small manufacturers have increased the area's economic opportunities.

 Every year, a number of families that were displaced by the Norris Dam project gather to revisit the sites of their old homes while the lake is at its lowest point.

WELCOME TO TENNESSEE

COUNTY CURIOSITIES

There are 62 counties on average in each of the 48 American states that divide their land into these forms of government. While Tennessee is far from the biggest state, ranking as the 36th largest, it has more than the national average when it comes to counties—there are 95 counties in Tennessee.

Made in Manhattan

Anderson County was founded on November 6, 1801. It's known for being one of the three main sites used during the Manhattan Project, the code name for an international project whose main goal was to be the first to develop the atomic bomb. The Manhattan Project operated in Anderson County near the city of Oak Ridge. It ran from 1941 to 1946, costing the U.S. government in the neighborhood of $2 billion and employing more than 130,000 people.

High Point

Benton County was created on December 19, 1835. Pilot Knob, the highest point in West Tennessee with an elevation of 650 feet above sea level, is located in Benton County.

Trail of Tears

Bradley County is the home of the historic Red Clay State Park. The park is significant because it is on the site formerly occupied by the Cherokee government before the Cherokee were forcibly removed from the area. The trail the Cherokee walked as they left their native land is named the Trail of Tears.

Coal County

Coal, in this case bituminous coal, is big money in Campbell County. In the early 1900s, Campbell County's bountiful coal production gave it the distinction of leading the state in this industry.

Waterfall Wonderland

With just seven square miles of water within the 348 square miles of Carter County, it's not exactly swimming with lake options. However, the county is noted for its many waterfalls, and it's also home to the Doe River Covered Bridge. Built in 1882 and spanning 134 feet across the Doe River, the bridge is believed to be the oldest of its kind in Tennessee.

Cover Up!

There are only three covered bridges still standing in Tennessee and another one of them is located in Dyer County. Built in 1904, the Emerison E. Parks Covered Bridge was added to the National Register of Historic Places in 1978.

Cumberland Gap

At least one million visitors pour through the Cumberland Gap every year, providing Clairborne County with its major tourist attraction.

Publishing Pride
Catherine Marshall made Cocke County famous when the McGraw-Hill Book Company of New York published her novel *Christy* in 1967. The book was inspired by different settings and characters around the county.

Devout Decatur
According to its website, Decatur County has more than 50 churches within its 345-square-mile area.

Sergeant York
Fentress County is famous for producing one of America's most renowned World War I heroes—Alvin York, who was born and lived in the area. The 1941 Academy Award–winning movie *Sergeant York* starred Gary Cooper in the titular role.

Simple Beauty
Franklin County's motto is, quite simply, "Beautiful."

Strawberry Fields
The West Tennessee Strawberry Festival draws crowds of as many as 100,000 people during its annual event.

Soup of the Day
Bradford, a community of Gibson County, is known as the "Doodle Soup Capital of the World." The origin of the soup is unknown, but it's thought that the spicy, vinegary soup made with pan drippings from cooked chicken was created by hungry Union soldiers during the Civil War. In this version of the story, the "Doodle" appellation is a reference to the song "Yankee Doodle Dandy."

You Say "Tomato"...

It's not all about the tomatoes in Grainger County, but the cherry-red crop certainly makes up a considerable portion of the county's agriculture industry. Other significant products grown in Grainger's 400 full-time farms include cattle, corn, beans and tobacco.

Terrific Topography

Hancock County is geologically varied, with mountains and valleys, farmland covering the undulating hillsides and the Clinch and Powell rivers. At 2618 feet above sea level, Clinch Mountain is the highest point in the county.

Hardeman Hardwood

Hardeman County is known as the "Hardwood Capital of Tennessee."

See You Again Soon

One local legend claims that if you dip your feet into any of the natural bodies of water in Hardin County, you will always come back for more.

Claim to Fame

Rogersville is the second oldest town in Tennessee. It is located in Hawkins County, where it serves as the county seat.

WELCOME TO TENNESSEE

Birth of the Blues

Sleepy John Estes, a blues musician born in Ripley is touted as one of Haywood County's "most notable residents," but he's certainly not the only "notable" performing artist to hail from Haywood. Another blues great, Hambone Willie Newbern, came from Haywood, and Tina Turner spent her childhood in the Haywood rural community of Nutbush.

Backing Barack

Houston County went down in history as one of the few Tennessee counties that backed Barack Obama's bid for the presidential election.

Sing It!
Singer-songwriter and musician Steve Earle immortalized Johnson County by making it the setting for his hit song, "Copperhead Road."

Laudable Lauderdale
There are quite a few notable folk that hail from Lauderdale County, like Alex Haley, the author of the epic novel *Roots*, and former Major League Baseball player Jim Hickman. It was also home to blues guitarist Sleepy John Estes and actor Miles O'Keeffe. Lauderdale's county seat is in Ripley, which is also the county's largest city.

Amish Country
One of the major tourist attractions in Lawrence County is the Old Order Amish community located in Ethridge, in the northern part of the county. The community began in 1944, has grown to a population of about 750 and operates as the "parent congregation" for newer Amish settlements.

Home of Jack Daniel's
Whiskey lovers might be interested to know that the Jack Daniel's Distillery—which was licensed in 1866, making it the oldest distillery in the U.S.—was originally located in Lincoln County. Lincoln County was founded in 1809, and although the distillery hasn't moved since it was erected, the county lines have, making it part of the newly formed Moore County in 1872.

Waterways
The two rivers running through Polk County offer residents and visitors several recreation options. The Ocoee River is a prime destination for whitewater slalom enthusiasts, and in 1996, when the Summer Olympic Games were held in

Atlanta, a mile-long portion of the Ocoee River served as the whitewater course. Polk County's other river, the Hiwassee River, runs a little slower and is used for recreational rafting and tubing.

Family Friendly
Putnam County prides itself on having "low crime, low property taxes and a county full of friendly caring people," making it "one of the best places in the country to live and raise a family."

Outdoor Extravaganza
Hiking is a big attraction for outdoor enthusiasts living in or visiting Rhea County. With such a wide and varied topography, there are many wilderness areas offering great hiking trails as well as waterways offering kayakers lots of courses to run.

New Discoveries
The first explorer to forge through the untamed wilderness west of North Carolina was Peter Avery. The hunter had been commissioned by the state of North Carolina to explore the area, and he came back with stories about rich soil, majestic mountains and cool-running streams in the region that would eventually become Roane County.

Whiskey Country
Whiskey flowed far and wide from the more than 75 distilleries operating in Robertson County. Sometime around 1820, tobacco became another major agriculture industry.

Great Scott!
What eventually became Scott County saw its first white settlers around 1778, though it wasn't until three-quarters of a century later, in 1849, that Scott County was officially founded.

Native American Legacy

Sequatchie County is named after the Sequatchie Valley, which comprises 250 square miles worth of the 266 square miles that makes up the county. The Sequatchie Valley was named in honor of the Cherokee chief of the same name.

The winding Mississippi River wends its way throughout the southern states, passing Memphis along the way, making the thriving city a logical place to establish a port. According to the International Port of Memphis, it is the "second largest inland port on the shallow draft portion of the Mississippi River, and the fourth largest inland port in the United States."

Stories and Songs from Sevier

Fans of the Coen brothers' movie *No Country For Old Men* will have heard of Cormack McCarthy, the author of the book that inspired the movie. More than three decades earlier, he wrote another book, *Child of God*, using Sevier County as its setting.

The city of Gatlinburg is also located in Sevier County and is the setting for the father-and-son showdown in Johnny Cash's hit song "A Boy Named Sue."

This Old House

Davies Manor Plantation, a two-story log-and-chink home located in Shelby County, was built some time before 1831, when additions were made to the original one-room home. It's believed by some historians to be the oldest house in the county.

An Inconvenient Truth?

One of Smith County's celebrity residents is none other than former vice president, Al Gore.

Switching Sides
Politics has taken an interesting turn of late in Stewart County. Traditionally a Democratic county, 2008 Republican presidential candidate John McCain pulled in 53.7 percent of the vote. It was the first time since 1968 that a Republican won in Stewart County.

United in Union
Entertainers Roy Acuff, Chet Atkins, Kenny Chesney and Carl Smith, along with fashion designer Jason Taylor and Jake Butcher, a one-time banker and politician convicted of fraud, all made their home in Union County at one time or another.

Community-minded County
The Van Buren County Chamber of Commerce makes a bold statement when it comes to the economy of its beautiful county: "There are no multimillion-dollar corporations pouring dollars into our community nor determining the destiny of Van Buren County…you won't find a Starbucks on our corners because we support local business development and growth." What they do have in Van Buren County are community-minded residents who believe in the value of friends and family and who reach out to help each other live well in the natural beauty that surrounds them.

Going Batty
Hubbard's Cave, one of the world's "most important bat hibernation sites," is located in Warren County.

Miss USA
Amy Colley, Miss Tennessee USA 2005, hails from Washington County.

Battle Ground
There were three main battles fought in the area of Williamson County during the Civil War—the Battle of Franklin, the

Battle of Brentwood and the Battle of Thompson's Station. The Battle of Franklin was often referred to as "one of the bloodiest battles of the war."

Tragic Trail

From 1826 to 1828, a path was beaten through the Wilson County countryside as Native American tribes were forced to leave their homes in the South and were sent to other locations as far away as Oklahoma. The route they took is known as the Trail of Tears.

Size-wise

- With a total land area of 474 square miles, Bedford County occupies a mere 1.1 percent of the entire state, making it one of Tennessee's smallest counties. And yet, according to statistics from 2007, the county boasts 1554 farms, occupying 231,206 acres of farmland and giving it an eighth place ranking among Tennessee counties.

- Cannon County is a tiny blip in middle Tennessee, measuring about 266 square miles. Perhaps there's a ditch or a dugout located somewhere in the count to account for the 0.02 percent that is covered in water.

- There are 7794 people in Clay County, according to 2008 estimates. With a total land area of 236 square miles, this makes the county comfortably roomy with only 33 people every square mile.

- With a population of 545,524, Nashville is the second largest city in Tennessee. It is also the Davidson County seat. Davidson County is also significant in that it is Middle Tennessee's oldest county.

- Of the 361 square miles that make up Grundy County, only 0.6 square miles is composed of water. Based on 2007 estimates, there are 14,275 people who live in the county.

- According to 2008 population estimates by the U.S. Census Bureau, there are approximately 332,848 people living in Hamilton County, which translates into about 578 persons per square mile.

- There are about 19,800 people living in Morgan County. Its largest city, with a population around 3000, is Oliver Springs, a city that is actually shared between three counties: Morgan, Anderson and Roane. Warburg, a town of about 928 according to 2008 estimates, is the county seat.

- At only 175 square miles, Pickett County is one of Tennessee's smallest counties. About 5000 people live there, but the area's population balloons significantly during the summer thanks to the many resorts in the Twin Lakes area.

- With a 2009 population estimate of 100,798, Rutherford's Chamber of Commerce claims that their county is the "fastest growing county in Tennessee."

- Population-wise, Sullivan County is the sixth largest in the state.

- According to 2008 estimates, there were 33,375 residents in Weakley County, which has shown a 4.4 percent decline in population since the year 2000.

The state of Tennessee was home to two other counties during its long history. Tennessee County was formed in 1788 and dissolved in 1796 when Tennessee became a state. Part of it became Montgomery County, and the remainder became part of Robertson County. James County was established in 1870 but was dissolved in 1919, and its lands became part of Hamilton County.

WELCOME TO TENNESSEE

Named After

- Blount County prides itself in being one of the state's oldest counties. It was created in 1795, the 10th county given the nod by the territorial legislature, and was named after Governor William Blount.

- Chester County was founded on March 1, 1879. The original name that was bandied about for the new county was Wisdom County. Eventually, the name Chester was chosen in honor of Colonel Robert I. Chester, a state legislator from Jackson. Cotton farming led the economy in the early years of the county's formation.

- Coffee County was established in 1836 and was named after General John Coffee. As of this writing, the county boasts nine Century Farms: the Beckman Farm, Brown Dairy Farm, Carden Ranch, Crouch-Ramsey Farm, The Homestead Farm, Jacobs Farm, Long Farm, Thomas Farm and the oldest of the bunch, Shamrock Acres, established in 1818.

- As the song goes, Davy Crockett was the "king of the wild frontier." But he was more than just a soldier and frontiersman—he also served as a member of the U.S. House of Representatives. It makes sense that the soldier was honored by having a county named after him, and in 1871, Crockett County was born.

- Dickson County was formed on October 25, 1803, and is named after William Dickson, a Nashville physician and statesman. What's been called a "Victorian Italianate-style mansion," originally built as a summer house, is the only surviving 19th-century mansion in Dickson County. It was once owned by James and Florence Drouillard and is currently operated as a retreat and conference centre.

- The Marquis de la Fayette, noted French hero of the American Revolution, was recognized for his efforts when Fayette County was named in his honor on September 29, 1824.

- Named after Hezekiah Hamblen, an early settler in the area, Hamblen County was founded in 1870.

- Having a future president hail from your state is certainly something to take pride in, but when he hails from your county, there's just one thing to do about it—rename the county after him! And that's exactly what folks from Jackson County did when they created the county in 1801 and named it after Andrew Jackson.

- U.S. Secretary of War Henry Knox must have been a pretty popular guy—he has nine different counties across the United States named after him. One of those counties is Knox County, established on June 11, 1792. Knox County was one of eight Tennessee counties created when the area was still under territorial administration.

- The Chickasaw Indians were the original occupants of the lands that now make up Tipton County. The county was founded on October 23, 1823, and is named after Jacob Tipton.

- Unicoi County has an interesting name whose roots, it is believed, stem from the Native American tradition. In particular, it's thought the name comes from the Cherokee word *u'nika*, meaning "white, fog-like or fog-draped."

WELCOME TO TENNESSEE

NUMBING NUMBERS AND NUGGETS

Don't Do Drugs

From backwoods distilleries to cocaine country stars, Tennessee has a long and storied history with drugs and alcohol. Like folks in the rest of the United States, Tennesseans seek out altered states of consciousness in order to wind down or to get all wound up. From the excesses of the rich and famous to the production of one of the world's greatest alcoholic beverages, for every Tennessean who beats the Bible there is another one who tips the bottle.

Here are some interesting facts about imbibing in the Volunteer State:

- ☞ Recent statistics show that an approximately 329,000 Tennesseans have a problem with alcohol abuse or dependence, while about 155,000 have an abuse, dependence or addiction problem involving one or more illicit drugs.

- ☞ Robert Mitchum's 1958 film *Thunder Road* featured the macho leading man as a moonshine runner evading authorities on a run to Memphis.

- Studies show that approximately 316,000 people in Tennessee who need treatment for alcohol abuse are not receiving it. The same lack of care exists for 146,000 individuals who are in need of rehabilitation for drug dependencies and addiction.

- Recent statistics show that the need for rehabilitation and care for individuals with drug and alcohol addiction is on the rise in Tennessee. Between 1995 and 2005, admissions to rehab programs in Tennessee rose from 9510 to 11,730.

- Most Tennesseans who enter rehab are suffering from alcohol problems. The second most popular drug of choice among rehabilitation admissions is crack cocaine.

- Heroin, tranquilizers and PCP are rarities in rehabilitation admissions in Tennessee.

- The alcohol and drug statistics in the state aren't great, and the trend seems to be on the increase: 8.4 percent of Tennesseans are currently dependent on or abusing an illicit drug or alcohol; 10.3 percent of Tennesseans use marijuana, while 2.3 percent use cocaine; and 5.5 percent of Tennesseans report the non-medical use of pain relievers.

- As in the rest of the United States, the abuse of prescription drugs is the most alarming statistic on the rise, especially among young people. In a 2005 study, 318,000 Tennesseans reported the non-medical use of prescription psychotherapeutic drugs, and 231,000 admitted to the non-medical use of pain relievers, though only 12,000 reported the use of methamphetamines.

- In 2009, the Tennessee General Assembly revised a law that limited the distillation of drinkable spirits to only three counties in the state—the new law graciously allows for distilleries in 41 counties. The good news is that this change is expected to create a number of new brands of Tennessee whiskey.

WELCOME TO TENNESSEE

☛ In 2007, authorities busted a marijuana grow-operation in Tennessee's Trousdale County. A hidden passage underneath a million-dollar residential home led into an underground cave complex that included offices, a bathroom, a full kitchen, air conditioning and over 1000 green plants being readied for the market. The site has since become known as the "Great Tennessee Pot Cave."

WELCOME TO TENNESSEE

SEX AND THE LAW
Below the Belt

For better or worse, drugs, alcohol and sex are usually regular bedfellows (please excuse the pun), so what is the state of sex in Tennessee? What rights do gay, lesbian, bisexual and transgender (GLBT) citizens have in the Volunteer State? How easy is it to obtain birth control or to get an abortion? What is the legal age of consent? Keep your pants on! Here's a treasure trove of ticklish tips and naughty nibblets to show you what's going on below the Bible Belt in the state of Tennessee:

- The legal age of consent in Tennessee is 18—anyone 17 or younger is considered a minor. Although pregnancy, legal emancipation, marriage and other extenuating circumstances can cloud the issue, the rule of thumb is to respect the age of 18 as sacrosanct.

- Tennesseans under 18 seeking an abortion must have parental consent from at least one parent or guardian. A judicial bypass can be sought in special cases where parental consent is not possible or in the case of a medical emergency.

- Teens are subject to a two-day waiting period before they can receive an abortion.

- There is no minimum age limit for the purchase of condoms in Tennessee.

- People 17 and older can buy emergency contraception over the counter. Teens, however, are required to get a prescription for these controversial "morning after" pills.

- Tennessee law requires sex education programs in public schools, and people of any age can receive confidential testing for STDs and AIDS.

- Tennessee schools don't have Safe Schools laws to specifically protect GLBT teens from harassment, but many school districts have adopted their own version of the Safe Schools policy.

- Statutory rape in Tennessee is defined as an act that takes place between a victim who is between 13 and 17 years of age and a rapist who is at least four years older.

- Spousal rape is a Class C felony in Tennessee.

- Like most states, Tennessee had a number of so-called "sodomy laws" for a very long time. These laws sought to limit acceptable sexual behavior in order to effectively criminalize homosexuality. Tennessee wisely cleared these laws from the books in 1996, seven years before the U.S. Supreme Court struck down all such laws across the country. Before 1996, almost all sexual expressions, save for male-female genital contact, were technically illegal in Tennessee.

- If both parents or guardians consent, Tennesseans as young as 16 are permitted to get married.

- No one younger than 13 can legally consent to sex in Tennessee.

- After the Civil War, Tennessee implemented legislation to keep whites from marrying African Americans. Constitutional barriers to interracial marriage were done away with in 1977.

WELCOME TO TENNESSEE

GAY COUPLES BY THE NUMBERS

Gay and Friendly
Although Tennessee is overwhelmingly heterosexual in its coupling habits, the state ranks more favorably than one might think as a place that gay couples have chosen to call home:

Tennessee total population: 5,689,283 (Tennessee ranks 16th in the U.S.)

Total same-sex couples: 10,189 (Tennessee ranks 18th in the U.S.)

People in same-sex couples: 0.36 percent (Tennessee ranks 31st in the U.S.)

Percentage of male couples: 4 percent (Tennessee ranks 19th in the U.S.)

Percentage of female couples: 4 percent (Tennessee ranks 34th in the U.S.)

WELCOME TO TENNESSEE

TENNESSEE ON TAP

While the roots of beer can be traced at least back to around 7000 BC, the modern rise of artisanal microbreweries in America only began about 25 years ago. Starting in the 1980s, the microbrewery movement introduced handcrafted beers to an audience that was increasingly drawn to the quality and diversity of these tasty new offerings, choosing them over the low priced and mega-marketed big commercial breweries. Tennessee claims a number of its own microbreweries, making the state not only a great place for beer lovers, but for all lovers of handcrafted, quality food and drink, as well as those who value some local character in the communities where they live and visit. Here's a list of Tennessee's best brews.

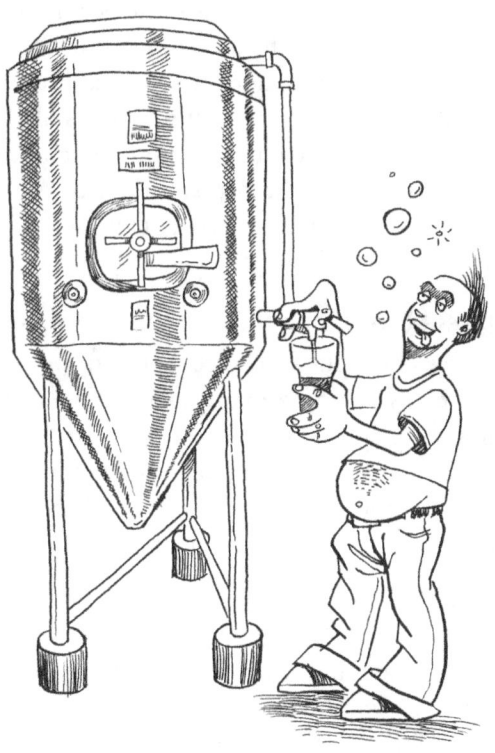

Big River

Big River has brewpub locations in Nashville and Buena Vista, Florida, but the beer brand calls Chattanooga home. One of Tennessee's most recognized beer labels, Big River is an award-winning brewer that prides itself on its adherence to the tried-and-true, centuries-old German beer purity laws, which limit the number of beer-making ingredients to barley, hops, water and yeast. Big River is also unique in that most of its beers are bottom-fermented, longer-aged lagers as opposed to the ales that most microbreweries produce. Big River's Czech Lager is a popular award winner.

Blackhorse

First opened in 1992, this downtown Clarksville brewpub is a popular local hangout and a must-taste beer producer in the Volunteer State. Although the pub also sells liquor and wine, its beer is the obvious attraction, and the Blackhorse beer selection isn't wanting for variety. With flavors like Raspberry, Vanilla Cream Ale and Coalminer's Stout, it can be hard to pick a favorite. However, the Barnstormer Red Ale is the Blackhorse's flagship brew and a consistent hit with Tennessee beer lovers.

Sophisticated Otter

East Tennessee's brewpub of choice, Sophisticated Otter, is located in the East Tennessee state college town of Johnson City. Although the pub can have as few as four beers on tap at a time, the popular spot has built a solid reputation based on its consistently scrumptious India Pale Ale and Porter selections. Their Pumpkin Ale is an autumn favorite.

Boscos

Billed as "the restaurant for beer lovers," Bosco's brewpub locations are distinguished by their food menus that are jam-packed with delicious offerings that go way beyond traditional pub grub—however, it's the beer that keeps Bosco's patrons coming back. With locations in Nashville, Memphis and Franklin, Bosco's is one of the brewers responsible for igniting microbrewery fever in the Volunteer State. While Bosco's offers a large variety of seasonal beers, its always-available house offerings like the Famous Flaming Stone and Bombay India Pale Ale are consistent favorites. If you are crazy for hops-heavy ales, Bosco's Hop God is not to be missed.

Smoky Mountain Brewery
The microbrewery that supplies the Copper Cellar restaurant group, Smoky Mountain Brewery has locations in Knoxville, Pigeon Forge and Gatlinburg. Although Smoky Mountain isn't one of the more popular names you'll hear in Tennessee's brewing circles, the label's products are consistently good, and their Bock, Helles and German Pilsner are starting to build this brewery a big reputation.

Blackstone
Located near Vanderbilt University in Nashville, Blackstone is a brewery and restaurant that many Music City beer lovers call home. Established in 1994, Blackstone was one of the first brewpubs in the city, and its ongoing success can be attributed to the tasty brews it creates onsite. Blackstone's seasonal offerings like Irish Stout and India Pale Ale bring connoisseurs back time and again to try the latest liquid treats. However, for regulars, house favorites like the St. Charles Porter and the Chaser Pale are tough to beat.

Yazoo
The latest brewery to bubble up in Nashville, Yazoo has quickly established itself as one of Music City's best brews. At their current location—the brewery will be moving to larger facilities in 2010—Yazoo treats their beer like wine, serving pints in their tasting room with pairings of artisan breads and cheeses. Everyone has their favorites, but the Pale Ale and the Dos Perros

pints are always popular. Yazoo's Hefeweizen won the gold medal at the Great American Brewers Festival in 2004.

Tips for Tennessean Tipplers

For some Tennesseans, enjoying a drink goes hand in hand with breaking the law. As with many of the southern states, Tennessee has its share of legendary—and more contemporary—stories about moonshiners and bootleggers—however, the two terms are often confused. A "bootlegger" is simply a businessman operating in the margins of the black market, whereas a "moonshiner" is something of an alchemist:

- **Moonshiner:** Someone who illegally distills his own liquor. This high-alcohol potion is usually coaxed out of corn mash using a small, homemade still. The term is thought to come from the clandestine, nocturnal habits of these distillers and delivery drivers, who prefer to work in the dark of night.

- **Bootlegger:** Tennessee has a number of "dry counties." In these communities, the sale of all liquor, wine and beer is absolutely prohibited. In fact, the state of Tennessee is dry by default—communities must decide to sell alcohol, not ban the practice. Most counties do sell alcohol, but Campbell, Cumberland, Hancock, Sevier and White are all dry counties, and the city of Lynchburg in Moore County is also dry, despite the fact that it's the home of the Jack Daniel's distillery. In a dry county, there is a ton of money to be made from bringing these forbidden fruits within reach of friends and neighbors who might fancy a wetter whistle. A bootlegger will visit a neighboring "wet" county to load up on legally sold alcohol, only to return to his dry county to resell the booty at a premium price.

TENNESSEE EATS

Like most regions of the country, the South has its own ideas about what makes a good meal. Pulling from local ingredients and long-standing traditions, here are a few appetizers that will give you a taste of what's for dinner in the Volunteer State.

All You Can Eat

A "meat-and-three" is a home-style buffet restaurant. The appellation refers to the usual daily special, which includes one meat dish with three sides. Commonly, this type of restaurant serves fried chicken, roast beef, fried shrimp or chicken and dumplings, along with sautéed greens, corn, mashed potatoes, black-eyed peas, macaroni and cheese and a number of other sides. Of course, when you visit a meat-and-three, be sure to save room for dessert!

Teatime

Tennesseans need to beat the heat in the summer, and they've come up with a variety of tasty solutions. For instance, iced tea in Tennessee comes in three distinct varieties: plain, sweet (with a "healthy" heaping of sugar) and fruit tea, which is usually a combination of sweet tea and orange juice, as well as other juices and spices depending on the recipe.

Lucky Peas

Black-eyed peas are edible beans that are popular in Tennessee and a staple in most Southern cooking. The peas are usually prepared with pork to add flavor. Jewish traditions around the world consider the eating of black-eyed peas to be good luck during New Year's celebrations. This tradition is followed by most Tennesseans as well, regardless of their religious affiliations.

Some Like It Hot

Hot chicken is a local specialty in Nashville. The fiery fowl is traditionally dredged in a buttermilk batter along with an infernal amount of cayenne pepper before it is pan-fried. Nashville is also the home of a related "hot fish" phenomenon, in which a fillet of catfish or whiting is treated in the same manner and served in a white-bread sandwich with mustard and onions. "Nashville Hot Chicken" has been listed as a menu item in restaurants as far north as Michigan.

Good on the Grill

Memphis barbecue is famous all over the world, and the recipe is as distinctive as the city it is named for. Memphis makes both dry-seasoned and "wet" pork ribs, topped with a sweet, tomato-based sauce. There is also a pulled- or chopped-pork sandwich, topped with coleslaw and served on a hamburger bun. Memphis is the home to the Memphis in May World Championship Barbecue Cooking Contest, the largest barbecue cooking contest in the world according to the *Guinness Book of Records*.

TENNESSEE WHISKEY

Outside the less-than-legal activities of bootleggers and moonshiners, Tennessee is home to two world-renowned distilleries that produce Tennessee whiskey: George Dickel and Jack Daniel's. These are the only brands that can claim the name "Tennessee whiskey": a sour mash, American whiskey that is filtered through maple charcoal before being cask-aged. This technique is known as the Lincoln County Process, named for the original location of the Jack Daniel's distillery.

It Came from Cascade Hollow

George Dickel's tradition of creating fine Tennessee whiskey began in 1870, when Dickel used water from the Cascade Springs to fill his first bottle of amber delight. Although it may be difficult to find the tiny 'burg of Cascade Hollow on a road map, you can rest assured that about halfway between Nashville and Chattanooga, tucked away on the Highland Rim of the Cumberland Plateau, Tennessee's chilly, clear spring water is being transformed into one of only two brands in the world that can claim the name "Tennessee whiskey."

Like all Tennessee whiskey, the Dickel brand is made from a sour mash of corn, barley and rye and then filtered through maple charcoal before it reaches the bottle. Dickel also adds a step in which the liquor is chilled before it reaches the charcoal mellowing vat. This technique is based on Dickel's assertion that his winter-weather creations were smoother than those distilled in warmer months—it's thought that the lower temperature of the water filters out oils and acids that detract from the whiskey's mellow flavor. Either way, this smoother flavor profile inspired Dickel to call his creation "Tennessee whisky," dropping the "e" in whiskey, thereby creating a connection between his product and the Scotch whisky tradition.

WELCOME TO TENNESSEE

The House that Jack Built

One of the best-selling liquors in the world, Jack Daniel's Tennessee whiskey has brought the taste of the Volunteer State to generations of strong-drink lovers from Western Europe to Eastern Asia for more than 100 years. The Jack Daniel's Distillery is the oldest registered distillery in the country—the facility still stands in the same place where Jack made his original batch of whiskey.

The first stop on the distillery tour finds visitors standing inside the cave where Jack collected the water for his first batch of beverages. This is also the location of one of the mysteries in a process that is full of mysteries: you see, the water in the cave flows at 800 gallons a minute, 365 days a year. The temperature of the water is a constant 56°F and it is virtually free of iron. This one-of-a-kind water is credited for the whiskey's smooth flavor, but the stream's origin is unknown. Although there have been multiple attempts to find the source of the strange spring, its bubbling beginnings have yet to be located.

Jack's Life

Jasper "Jack" Newton Daniel is generally thought to have been born in 1850, though the details of the whiskey inventor's early years are as confusing as many of the other mysteries surrounding the brand. If the date of 1850 is correct, then the distillery's agreed-upon founding date of 1866 seems odd, as that would mean that Daniel was only 16 when he began his whiskey empire. Another possible birthdate finds Daniel being born in 1846, while other sources claim that the distillery was founded in 1875. Part of the confusion may be attributable to a courthouse fire that seems to have destroyed Daniel's birth records. Daniel was also blessed with 12 brothers and sisters, so perhaps even his own mother and father had trouble keeping track of birthdays! When he was still a young boy, Jack left home to be raised by Dan Call, a family friend. Call was both a Lutheran minister and the proud owner of a whiskey still. Call taught Jack everything he knew about making whiskey, and when the preacher decided to dedicate the rest of his life to his ministry, Jack inherited his original still.

Jack's Whiskey

Jack Daniel's premium Black Label brand is known around the globe. The whiskey is recognizable by its distinctive square bottle and its simply styled black label. Originally, the whiskey came in earthenware jugs. When Daniel switched to glass to keep up with changing tastes, he insisted that his bottle had to be as distinctive as his whiskey. In 1895, Daniels chose his unique square bottle with a fluted neck and the style has stuck ever since. The number "7" on the label is another one of the brand's biggest mysteries—no one knows for sure what the significance of the number is, but, of course, many rumors abound. One tale says that Jack had seven girlfriends. Another says that Daniel's handwritten J's looked like 7's. Some say that Daniel discovered his legendary blend on his seventh attempt to perfect the whiskey. Or perhaps Daniel—like all gamblers—simply felt the number was lucky. All these years later, the mystery—not to mention the whiskey—still remains.

Death of a Legend

Legend has it that Jack Daniel kicked his heavy, iron safe in frustration after forgetting the combination one morning and broke his toe. The resulting injury led to a case of blood poisoning that took Daniel's life in 1911. Those who seek out Jack's final resting place will find it in the Lynchburg town cemetery. The large headstone is flanked by two white chairs, supposedly there to support all the local women who were devastated by Mr. Daniel's passing.

DID YOU KNOW?

In 1892, Jack Daniel formed the Silver Coronet Band to draw crowds to Lynchburg Square, where he operated two saloons—the Red Dog and the White Rabbit.

WELCOME TO TENNESSEE

10. You haven't lived until you've tried Memphis barbecue!

9. Nicole Kidman lives here, and so should you!

8. Nashville is one of the best places in the world for a music lover!

7. Get away from that horrible northern winter!

6. Tennessee's cost of living is one of the lowest in the country!

5. Tennessee's moderate climate makes the state a year-round sportsman's paradise!

4. Tennessee is still in the process of discovering itself, and Nashville is one of the fastest-growing cities in the country!

3. Tennessee is a leader in health care. This is great news for medical professionals and patients alike!

2. With Al Gore living in Nashville, Tennessee may be one of the only states that's safe from global warming!

1. Southern hospitality is alive and well in Tennessee—if you come visit, we know you won't ever want to leave!

ABOUT THE ILLUSTRATORS

Craig Howrie

Craig is a self-taught artist. His line art has been used in local businesses' private events as well as a local comic book art anthology. This is the second book he has illustrated for Blue Bike Books. He is also a songwriter working feverishly at a project that will hopefully see the light of day within the next decade or so…

Roger Garcia

Roger Garcia was born El Salvador and came to North America with his parents at the age of seven. Because of the language barrier, he had to find a way to communicate with other kids. That's when he discovered the art of tracing, and it wasn't long before he had mastered this highly skilled technique. He taught himself to paint and sculpt, and then in high school and college, Roger skipped class to hide in the art room all day in order to further explore his talent. Roger's work can be seen in many other Blue Bike books.

ABOUT THE ILLUSTRATORS

Peter Tyler

Peter is a recent graduate of the Vancouver Film School's Visual Art and Design and Classical animation programs. Though his ultimate passion is in film-making, he is also intent on developing his draftsmanship and storytelling, with the aim of using those skills in future filmic misadventures.

Roly Wood

Roly grew up in Indian River, Ontario. He has worked in Toronto as a freelance illustrator, and was also employed in the graphic design department of a landscape architecture firm specializing in themed retail and entertainment design. In 2004, he wrote and illustrated a historical comic book set in Lang Pioneer Village near Peterborough. Roly currently lives and works as a freelance illustrator in Calgary, Alberta, with his wife, Kerri, and their dog, Hank.

ABOUT THE AUTHORS

J. Ernest Nolan

Tennessee resident J. Ernest Nolan is a graduate of Michigan State University, where he studied mass communications and culture. He is an award-winning fiction writer, poet and journalist. His work has appeared in a number of online and print publications. He lives in a 100-year-old apartment in Nashville within walking distance of his favorite coffeehouse.

Lisa Wojna

Lisa is the author of six other non-fiction books for Blue Bike Books, including *Book of Babies* and *Bathroom Book of Christmas Trivia*. She's also the author of four other non-fiction books and has co-authored more than a dozen others. She has worked in the community newspaper industry as a writer and journalist and has traveled all over Canada from the windy prairies of Manitoba to northern British Columbia and even to the wilds of Africa. Although writing and photography have been a central part of her life for as long as she can remember, it's the people behind every story that are her motivation and give her the most fulfillment.

www.ingramcontent.com/pod-product-compliance
Lightning Source LLC
LaVergne TN
LVHW051828080426
835512LV00018B/2778